Beyond Sunday —Copyright ©2024 by Tony Tice
Published by UNITED HOUSE Publishing

All rights reserved. No portion of this book may be reproduced or shared in any form–electronic, printed, photocopied, recording, or by any information storage and retrieval system, without prior written permission from the publisher. The use of short quotations is permitted.

The Holy Bible, English Standard Version. ESV® Text Edition: 2016. Copyright © 2001 by Crossway Bibles, a publishing ministry of Good News Publishers.

ISBN: 978-1-952840-54-8

UNITED HOUSE Publishing
Waterford, Michigan
info@unitedhousepublishing.com
www.unitedhousepublishing.com

Cover Layout and Interior Design:
Matt Russell, Marketing Image, mrussell@marketing-image.com

Printed in the United States of America
2024—First Edition

SPECIAL SALES
Most UNITED HOUSE books are available at special quantity discounts when purchased in bulk by corporations, organizations, and special-interest groups. For information, please e-mail orders@unitedhousepublishing.com

Beyond Sunday

BOOK OF JAMES BIBLE STUDY

Tony Tice

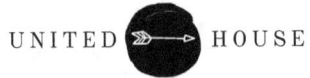

Table of Contents

Introduction 9

Trials (James 1:1-12)

Day 1 – James 1:1 15
Day 2 – James 1:2-4 19
Day 3 – James 1:5-8 23
Day 4 – James 1:9-11 27
Day 5 – James 1:12 31

Sin (James 1:13-27)

Day 6 – James 1:13-16 37
Day 7 – James 1:17-18 41
Day 8 – James 1:19-21 45
Day 9 – James 1:22-25 49
Day 10 – James 1:26-27 53

Partiality (James 2:1-13)

Day 11 – James 2:1-4 59
Day 12 – James 2:5-7 63
Day 13 – James 2:8-9 67
Day 14 – James 2:10-11 71
Day 15 – James 2:12-13 75

Faith and Works (James 2:14-26)

Day 16 – James 2:14 81
Day 17 – James 2:15-17 85
Day 18 – James 2:18-19 89
Day 19 – James 2:20-23 93
Day 20 – James 2:24-26 97

Words (James 3:1-12)

Day 21 – James 3:1-2 103
Day 22 – James 3:3-5 107
Day 23 – James 3:6-8 111
Day 24 – James 3:9-10 115
Day 25 – James 3:11-12 119

Wisdom (James 3:13-18)

Day 26 – James 3:13 125
Day 27 – James 3:14-15 129
Day 28 – James 3:16 133
Day 29 – James 3:17 137
Day 30 – James 3:18 141

Worldiness (James 4:1-12)

Day 31 – James 4:1-3 147
Day 32 – James 4:4-5 151
Day 33 – James 4:6-8 155
Day 34 – James 4:9-10 159
Day 35 – James 4:11-12 163

God's Will (James 4:13-17)

Day 36 – James 4:13 169
Day 37 – James 4:14 173
Day 38 – James 4:15 177
Day 39 – James 4:16 181
Day 40 – James 4:17 185

Materialism and Patience (James 5:1-12)

Day 41 – James 5:1-3 191
Day 42 – James 5:4-6 195
Day 43 – James 5:7-8 199
Day 44 – James 5:9-11 203
Day 45 – James 5:12 207

Prayer (James 5:13-20)

Day 46 – James 5:13-14 213
Day 47 – James 5:15 217
Day 48 – James 5:16 221
Day 49 – James 5:17-18 225
Day 50 – James 5:19-20 229

Notes 233
About the Author 235

Introduction

Our faith is so much more than a service we attend on Sunday morning. It's a 24/7 pursuit. It's a faith beyond Sunday. In many ways, our Christian life is measured more by what we do on Monday than by how we sing on Sunday.

Faith is more than lofty ideas. It's practical. It impacts how we think, how we talk, and how we interact with those around us. The gospel changes everything; it's supposed to anyway.

James is perhaps the most practical book of the entire Bible. It deals with everyday life. The author deals with things like trials, temptations, our speech, our relationships, and prayer.

It's not filled with hard-to-understand doctrine. James is blunt and to the point. He doesn't hold back. You don't leave your time in the book scratching your head, trying to figure out how to apply it.

This study is broken into ten main themes. It includes five days of study per theme. While the idea is to cover one theme each week, feel free to go at your own pace.

Each day ends with a few questions to help promote personal reflection. I'd encourage you not to skip this part. Reading God's Word *and* the study that goes with it is important. But, taking time to pause and ask how these truths apply to your life is also a very important part of your journey in this book.

As the author tells us in James 1:22, we are to "be doers of the word, and not hearers only." The goal is not to just read this study but to apply it to your life in a way that will help you grow in your relationship with God and others.

It's my prayer this study will be a tool the Holy Spirit uses to help you, as a Christ follower, have faith beyond Sunday.

Trials
James 1:1-12

¹James, a servant of God and of the Lord Jesus Christ, To the twelve tribes in the Dispersion: Greetings. ²Count it all joy, my brothers, when you meet trials of various kinds, ³for you know that the testing of your faith produces steadfastness. ⁴And let steadfastness have its full effect, that you may be perfect and complete, lacking in nothing. ⁵If any of you lacks wisdom, let him ask God, who gives generously to all without reproach, and it will be given him. ⁶But let him ask in faith, with no doubting, for the one who doubts is like a wave of the sea that is driven and tossed by the wind. ⁷For that person must not suppose that he will receive anything from the Lord; ⁸he is a double-minded man, unstable in all his ways. ⁹Let the lowly brother boast in his exaltation, ¹⁰and the rich in his humiliation, because like a flower of the grass he will pass away. ¹¹For the sun rises with its scorching heat and withers the grass; its flower falls, and its beauty perishes. So also will the rich man fade away in the midst of his pursuits. ¹²Blessed is the man who remains steadfast under trial, for when he has stood the test he will receive the crown of life, which God has promised to those who love him.

Day 1

¹James, a servant of God and of the Lord Jesus Christ, To the twelve tribes in the Dispersion: Greetings.
James 1:1

Let's begin by answering *who*. Who wrote this letter? This letter, of course, was written by James. But which James? James was a popular name in Bible times. There are numerous men named James in the New Testament. Two of the twelve disciples were named James—James the son of Alphaeus and James the son of Zebedee (and brother of John). And then there was James, the father of the disciple Jude. But none of these is the author of the letter.

This letter was most likely written by James, the half-brother of Jesus. What's interesting is that James did not believe Jesus was God during His earthly ministry (John 7:5). What caused James to become a believer? The resurrected Savior appeared to him (1 Corinthians 15:7). James grew deeply after Jesus appeared to him. Why? Because Jesus became more than a brother, He became his Lord. James would go on to become the leader of the church in Jerusalem.

> *Humble people aren't into names and titles, they simply see themselves as servants of God.*

Beyond Sunday

Historian Eusebius of Caesarea wrote James was known as "Old Camel Knees" because he prayed so often, he developed calluses on his knees. And notice the humility of James.
Instead of mentioning his relationship with Jesus, he simply refers to himself as "a servant of God and of the Lord Jesus Christ." Humble people aren't into names and titles, they simply see themselves as servants of God.

Tradition tells us James was martyred in 62 A.D. when he refused to renounce Christ. He was thrown from the top of the Temple. When that didn't kill him, he was beaten to death by clubs. James went from denying who Jesus was to refusing to deny who He was. What a great reminder for us that you never know what God can do in a life. Never stop praying for those in your life who don't know Jesus. Perhaps we need to develop some calluses on our knees from fervent and faith-filled praying!

Day 1

Day 1 Personal Reflection

How fervent in prayer are you for those far from God? Who are a couple of people you could pray for today?

Day 2

²Count it all joy, my brothers, when you meet trials of various kinds, ³for you know that the testing of your faith produces steadfastness. ⁴And let steadfastness have its full effect, that you may be perfect and complete, lacking in nothing.
James 1:2-4

Yesterday we looked at *who*, today we look at *why*. Why did James write this book? Understanding who he wrote it to will help us understand why. According to v. 1, James wrote the letter "to the twelve tribes in the Dispersion." The "twelve tribes" refers to the twelve tribes of Israel (which originate from the twelve sons of Jacob). In other words, James is writing, primarily, to a Jewish Christian audience.

James specifically writes to the Jews "in the Dispersion." The Greek word for "dispersed" is *diaspora* and simply means "scattered." These were Jews who had been scattered all over the world because of persecution. One of the reasons for this letter was to encourage believers facing difficult times. That's

> James isn't saying to take joy in the pain, he's saying to take joy in what the pain produces.

Beyond Sunday

something all of us can relate to.

And what, according to v. 2, are the encouraging words James offers the hurting? Be joyful with your trials. *Say what?* On the surface, this seems insensitive, like the person who thinks it's encouraging to tell a sufferer, "When life hands you a lemon, make lemonade."

James isn't saying to take joy in the pain; He's saying to take joy in what the pain produces. Or, should I say, what it *can* produce. Notice the process. When trials hit, recognize it's "the testing of your faith." It's been said that a faith that can't be tested can't be trusted. Faith muscles stretch through trials.

When we learn to endure the testing, it produces "steadfastness" in us. Think of steadfastness as "faith stretched out." Trials can develop a *stick-to-it-ness* kind of faith. And over time, the result is that we will be "perfect and complete, not lacking anything." Of course, we will never be perfect until heaven, but the idea is Christ-like maturity which leads to a life of contentment.

The question is, what matters more to us, character or comfort? If godly character is the answer, then we can have joy knowing what the trials will produce. Our outlook determines our outcome. How will you view the trials in your life?

Day 2

Day 2 Personal Reflection

Does comfort or character matter more to you? Are you seeing trials in your life from a Biblical perspective?

_____

_____

_____

_____

_____

_____

_____

_____

_____

_____

_____

_____

_____

Day 3

⁵If any of you lacks wisdom, let him ask God, who gives generously to all without reproach, and it will be given him. ⁶But let him ask in faith, with no doubting, for the one who doubts is like a wave of the sea that is driven and tossed by the wind. ⁷For that person must not suppose that he will receive anything from the Lord; ⁸he is a double-minded man, unstable in all his ways.
James 1:5-8

At first glance, these verses seem unrelated to James' instructions about trials. However, they are very much related. We need wisdom to know how to navigate through the difficult seasons of life. Wisdom is knowing how to live well. Trials are inevitable. The key to life is not avoiding them but learning how to live with them.

And here's the great news about wisdom . . . it wants to be found! It says in v. 5, if you lack wisdom, just ask, because God "gives generously." Proverbs 1:20 says, "Wisdom cries aloud in the streets, in the market she raises her voice." Ask and you shall receive! Wisdom comes

> *Trials are inevitable. The key to life is not avoiding them, but learning how to live with them.*

Beyond Sunday

from asking in prayer and when we seek it in God's Word.

There is a condition, however, found in v. 6. We must ask for wisdom "in faith, with no doubting." We must believe God wants to give us insight in the suffering. Without Biblical wisdom, we will bounce all over the place, spiritually and emotionally, or as James puts it, "driven and tossed by the wind."

James has strong words for the one who chooses not to believe God will give insight and guidance in our trials. James calls this person "double-minded" and "unstable." To be double-minded is to claim faith in God but, inwardly, to doubt Him and His Word. And when one doesn't address doubt, their spiritual life will be marked by instability, according to the end of v. 7.

You could say, if a person is to endure trials well, and experience Christ-like growth, they need to have a *persevering* heart (vs. 2-4) and a *believing* heart (vs. 5-8). Prayer is our greatest weapon to fight our temptation to give up. It's also our greatest weapon when we struggle with doubt. Throughout Scripture, we see a God who honors and responds to persistent, faith-filled praying. Are those the things that mark our prayer life?

Day 3

Day 3 Personal Reflection

What are some ways you are struggling with doubt? Are you consistently praying for wisdom to handle the aches and pains of life? If not, why do you think that is?

_____

_____

_____

_____

_____

_____

_____

_____

_____

_____

_____

_____

_____

_____

Day 4

⁹Let the lowly brother boast in his exaltation, ¹⁰and the rich in his humiliation, because like a flower of the grass he will pass away. ¹¹For the sun rises with its scorching heat and withers the grass; its flower falls, and its beauty perishes. So also will the rich man fade away in the midst of his pursuits.
James 1:9-11

We have seen, so far, that when we are facing trials in life, we need to have a persevering and believing heart. In today's verses, we see we need to also have a *humble* heart. James gives a contrast in these verses between the "lowly" and the "rich." He also gives what seems like a contradiction. The lowly should boast in their "exaltation" and the rich in their "humiliation."

We have to remember these verses were written within the context of the "testing of our faith." Individuals on both sides of the economic scale face trials. The rich are not immune. Andrew Carnegie, a wealthy industrialist from the 19th Century, once said, "Millionaires seldom smile."

> Don't think that having more will solve your problems.

These verses are not suggesting

that it's wrong to be blessed financially. However, the primary recipients of this letter were experiencing financial hardships because of their commitments to Christ. Many were ostracized from their community and it was affecting their livelihood.

For the "lowly" James is saying to remember the gospel, which should lead them to celebrate their spiritual "exaltation" (v. 9). Paul says in Ephesians 2:7 that God has "raised us up with him and seated us with him in the heavenly places." We have eternal riches, and that is worth celebrating, even when life is hard!

The challenge to those who put their hope in earthly riches is that it will eventually lead to "humiliation" (v. 10). James uses the example of a beautiful flower that eventually withers away. The stuff will eventually fade away, if not in this life, then in the one to come. And the harsh reminder that if one puts their hope in the things of this world, it will cost them their soul for all eternity.

There are a lot of possible applications in these verses. But here's just one: Don't think that having more will solve your problems. It may just give you more! We need to hold loosely to the things of this world but hold tightly to the eternal.

Day 4

Day 4 Personal Reflection

*How tightly are you holding to the stuff of this world?
How are you living with eternity in mind?*

Day 5

[12]Blessed is the man who remains steadfast under trial, for when he has stood the test he will receive the crown of life, which God has promised to those who love him.
James 1:12

There is something Christians, Jews, Buddhists, Hindus, Muslims, and Atheists have in common. They all want to be blessed. I certainly do, don't you? James tells us who can experience the blessed life in v. 12. And it's not what people would expect. The blessed life comes from trials. Yes, you read correctly. More specifically, though, it is how we *respond* to trials that lead to a blessed life.

The Greek word for "blessed" is *makarios*. It carries the idea of a happy, fulfilled life. To expand on that a bit, the blessed life is the joy that is produced when we experience God's favor in our lives. And according to James, that happens when we "remain steadfast" when the trials of life come our way.

> The next time you are going through a trial, don't be so quick to ask God to just get you through it. Ask Him to make something of you while you're in it.

Jesus used the same word for

Beyond Sunday

blessed in Matthew 5 when He talked about the Beatitudes. In v. 10 He said, "Blessed are those who are persecuted for righteousness' sake, for theirs is the kingdom of heaven." Remember, the trials for many of the letter's recipients were the result of persecution. James confirmed what Jesus said. You endure trials and persecution, and you will have true joy that circumstances can't take away.

Part of the reason you can have joy is because enduring trials helps make us more like Jesus. He uses trials to help refine our character. The next time you are going through a trial, don't be so quick to ask God to just get you through it. Ask Him to make something of you while you're in it.

And notice, in the verse, the reward won't just be a blessed life here on earth. James writes that we will receive the "crown of life." This is a metaphor for heaven. The ultimate prize for following after Jesus is the eternal reward of heaven. I don't think anyone enjoys trials, but if you let God stretch you in the suffering, He will grow you, He will bless you, and He will reward you with eternal glory!

Day 5

Day 5 Personal Reflection

When going through trials, do you ask God to just get you through it or do you ask Him to do something in you, while you're in it? What trial(s) are you facing now, and what could God be teaching you?

Sin
James 1:13-27

¹³*Let no one say when he is tempted, "I am being tempted by God," for God cannot be tempted with evil, and he himself tempts no one.* ¹⁴*But each person is tempted when he is lured and enticed by his own desire.* ¹⁵*Then desire when it has conceived gives birth to sin, and sin when it is fully grown brings forth death.* ¹⁶*Do not be deceived, my beloved brothers.* ¹⁷*Every good gift and every perfect gift is from above, coming down from the Father of lights, with whom there is no variation or shadow due to change.* ¹⁸*Of his own will he brought us forth by the word of truth, that we should be a kind of firstfruits of his creatures.* ¹⁹*Know this, my beloved brothers: let every person be quick to hear, slow to speak, slow to anger;* ²⁰*for the anger of man does not produce the righteousness of God.* ²¹*Therefore put away all filthiness and rampant wickedness and receive with meekness the implanted word, which is able to save your souls.* ²²*But be doers of the word, and not hearers only, deceiving yourselves.* ²³*For if anyone is a hearer of the word and not a doer, he is like a man who looks intently at his natural face in a mirror.* ²⁴*For he looks at himself and goes away and at once forgets what he was like.* ²⁵*But the one who looks into*

the perfect law, the law of liberty, and perseveres, being no hearer who forgets but a doer who acts, he will be blessed in his doing. [26] If anyone thinks he is religious and does not bridle his tongue but deceives his heart, this person's religion is worthless. [27] Religion that is pure and undefiled before God the Father is this: to visit orphans and widows in their affliction, and to keep oneself unstained from the world.

Day 6

¹³Let no one say when he is tempted, "I am being tempted by God," for God cannot be tempted with evil, and he himself tempts no one. ¹⁴But each person is tempted when he is lured and enticed by his own desire. ¹⁵Then desire when it has conceived gives birth to sin, and sin when it is fully grown brings forth death. ¹⁶Do not be deceived, my beloved brothers.
James 1:12

Everyone faces temptation. Even Jesus did when He walked the earth (Matthew 4). In v. 13, James said *when* not *if*. James wants his readers to know, first of all, God is never the source of temptation. He is not tempted by sin nor would He ever tempt us with sin. However, it's easy to think things like, *Why did God give me this weakness?* or *Why did God put me in this situation?* We must remember God may test us for good but He will never tempt us for evil.

James makes it clear in v. 14 that temptation comes from primarily two places: the desires that come from within and from Satan. The Greek word for "desire" in vs. 14-15 is *epithumia*, which means a craving but not

> Oftentimes, sin is taking a good desire but using it in an inappropriate way

necessarily an evil craving. Oftentimes, sin is taking a good desire but using it in an inappropriate way. Food is good, but we can become gluttonous. Sex in marriage is a gift from God, but we can commit sexual immorality.

Satan takes God-given desires and tempts us with them in ungodly ways. This is the first step of temptation. The next step, according to v. 15, is letting the temptation be "conceived," which is giving serious thought to the temptation. We begin to rationalize or justify it. When tempted, you and I can do one of two things. We can *feed* the temptation or we can *flee* from it.

If we feed the desire, the third step of temptation will be to "give birth to sin." We will violate God's Word, which can lead to the fourth step of sin becoming "fully grown." This means sin will have complete control over us. When this happens, it leads to the fifth step, which "brings forth death." Sin can destroy our lives and relationships.

It's been said that sin will take you farther than you want to go, keep you longer than you want to stay, and cost you more than you want to pay. How true that is. James ends with the plea, "do not be deceived" (v. 16). We must not let Satan deceive us. There is a high price to pay for sin. Let's flee, not feed temptation this week.

Day 6

Day 6 Personal Reflection

Are you feeding sin or fleeing from sin right now in your life? What would it look like to flee sin in your life?

_____

_____

_____

_____

_____

_____

_____

_____

_____

_____

_____

_____

Day 7

^{17}Every good gift and every perfect gift is from above, coming down from the Father of lights, with whom there is no variation or shadow due to change. ^{18}Of his own will he brought us forth by the word of truth, that we should be a kind of firstfruits of his creatures.
James 1:17-18

In the previous verses, we looked at the temptation of Satan. Today, we look at the goodness of God. We learn in v. 13 that God takes *no responsibility* for sin (nor should He), and in v. 17, we learn God takes *full responsibility* for every good thing (as He should). Our health. Our family. Our jobs. All graciously given to us by the "Father of lights."

Notice, He's not just our Father, He's our "Father of lights." What does this mean? This was an ancient Jewish title for God, emphasizing He is the creator of the world and the giver of light- the sun, moon, and stars. But unlike the sun, moon, and stars, there is "no variation or shadow due to change" with God.

> *Our lives are to represent the best of what God has created.*

God does not change (Malachi 3:6). It doesn't mean God is unmoved. God is a person who

Beyond Sunday

possesses emotions. We see in Luke 15, the father (which represents the Heavenly Father) running and embracing his prodigal son with compassion and joy. The Father is moved by His children! Let that soak into your soul today.

God is unchanging as it relates to His character. Even the godliest individual isn't 100% consistent in character. God is the only being that is perfect in conduct and character. He will always be loving. He will always be gracious. He will always be holy. He will always be faithful. We never have to worry about God disappointing His children.

Today's verses are intended to be a contrast to 13-16. In those verses, we discover Satan wants to take something from us. He wants to take our life! In today's verses, we discover God wants to give us something. The Father gives His children gifts!

The greatest gift we've been given, according to v. 18, is that "he brought us forth by the word of truth." This is a description of salvation. God has given us a new birth through the truth of God's Word. The truth is, Jesus died for sins and rose from the dead. The greatest gift indeed!

James closes out the verse by reminding us that the result of our salvation is we have become a kind of firstfruits of his creatures. In the Old Testament, the firstfruits were the first and the best of the harvested crops. Our lives are to represent the best of what God has created. In light of God's gift of salvation, may our lives reflect the firstfruits of all we have been given.

Day 7

Day 7 Personal Reflection

How often do you take time to thank the Father for the gifts He has given you? How does your life represent the best of what God has created?

Day 8

[19]Know this, my beloved brothers: let every person be quick to hear, slow to speak, slow to anger; [20]for the anger of man does not produce the righteousness of God. [21]Therefore put away all filthiness and rampant wickedness and receive with meekness the implanted word, which is able to save your souls.
James 1:19-21

In v. 18, James challenged believers to live like the firstfruits of his creatures, to represent the best of His creation. In vs. 19-21, James addresses behavior that does not represent the best in us. He begins with anger.

While there is such a thing as righteous anger, that's not what James is dealing with here. He's writing about the kind of anger that can destroy relationships. It's the "anger of man" that doesn't reflect the "righteousness of God." In v. 19, James gives three stages to follow.

Stage one is to be "quick to hear." Let's be honest, most of us are quick to speak and slow to hear. King Solomon wrote about the dangers of this in Proverbs 18:13: "If one gives an

> *There's a reason we've been given two ears and only one mouth!*

answer before he hears, it is his folly and shame." Many have gotten into trouble by not taking the time to truly listen to what a person is saying.

Stage two is to be "slow to speak," which isn't just about taking time before you talk. It carries the idea of processing what you've heard before opening your mouth. It's seeking to understand a person and what they're trying to communicate. There's a reason we've been given two ears and only one mouth!

When we truly listen to a person and try to really understand, it should help us with the third stage, which is to be "slow to anger." Proverbs 29:11 (NIV) says, "Fools give full vent to their rage, but the wise bring calm in the end." The fool gives into his anger; the wise tames his temper.

In v. 21, we see the primary theme for the second half of this chapter. It is to "receive with meekness the implanted word." We can't authentically live out our faith if we don't regularly embrace the Word of God.

This verse is connected to the previous verses. You can't have anger in your heart and still embrace the Word. The heart isn't in a healthy place to receive it. And it's not just anger. James says we have to put away "all filthiness" and "wickedness." It's been said that the Bible will keep us from sin or sin will keep us from the Bible. We must confess issues of the heart in order to humbly embrace God's holy Word.

Day 8

Day 8 Personal Reflection

Are you struggling with anger towards anyone? How are you addressing it? Are there any unconfessed areas of sin keeping you from fully embracing God's Word?

Day 9

^{22}But be doers of the word, and not hearers only, deceiving yourselves. ^{23}For if anyone is a hearer of the word and not a doer, he is like a man who looks intently at his natural face in a mirror. ^{24}For he looks at himself and goes away and at once forgets what he was like. ^{25}But the one who looks into the perfect law, the law of liberty, and perseveres, being no hearer who forgets but a doer who acts, he will be blessed in his doing.
James 1:22-25

We've all been deceived by someone at some point in our life. But the truth is, we can also deceive ourselves. James tells us how in v. 22. It's when we hear the Word of God but don't do what it says. How is that deceiving ourselves? It gives us a false sense of security.

We think we're good with God because we've read the Bible. Because we have head knowledge. And yet, we miss the truth by 18 inches—the distance between our head and our heart. The truth of God's Word must go from the head to the heart and, ultimately, to the feet. God

> *The truth of God's Word must go from the head to the heart and ultimately to the feet.*

is not honored by simply picking up the Bible. He is honored when we apply the Bible to our lives.

James is fond of metaphors. In vs. 23-24, he gives us one regarding a mirror. He talks about the person who looks at a mirror but doesn't make any adjustments that need to be made, like a hair out of place or a mark on the face. He compares this to a person who reads the Bible but makes no application or adjustment to their life. What a waste!

The person in v. 25 understands that the Bible is "perfect" and that it produces "liberty" and, therefore, applies God's Word to their life. Because it's perfect, we can put our full trust in it. The Word brings liberty to our lives. How so? It can free us from sinful behavior. It can free us from negative thought patterns. It can free us from unhealthy relationships.

When we truly believe God's Word, believe it enough to live out its truths in our lives, it will set us free to be all God created us to be. Jesus said in John 8:32, "You will know the truth, and the truth will set you free." But it's not just from knowing it, it's from living it. In addition, God promises we "will be blessed" in all we do. Let's not just read the Word, let's live it!

Day 9

Day 9 Personal Reflection

What things are keeping you from spending time in God's Word? How are you applying what you're reading?

_____

_____

_____

_____

_____

_____

_____

_____

_____

_____

_____

_____

_____

Day 10

²⁶If anyone thinks he is religious and does not bridle his tongue but deceives his heart, this person's religion is worthless. ²⁷Religion that is pure and undefiled before God the Father is this: to visit orphans and widows in their affliction, and to keep oneself unstained from the world.
James 1:26-27

We all had to take tests in school. Some of them included multiple-choice questions. Some included essay questions. Some fill-in-the-blank. And some were true or false questions. As James wraps up the first chapter, he mentions what is true and what is a false spirituality.

In v. 26 James says people who think they are spiritual, but don't control their tongues, have been deceived, and their faith is "worthless." Strong words from James. A person who doesn't tame the tongue reveals their heart issues. At least, that's what Jesus said in Matthew 12:33b: "For out of the abundance of the heart the mouth speaks."

Healthy words reflect a healthy heart. Unhealthy words reflect an unhealthy heart. And if we don't address the issues of the

> We have been saved to serve!

heart, our words will hurt those around us. It will lead to a worthless faith. James is not saying we are worthless, he's saying our faith is worthless or ineffective. James will come back to the topic of the tongue in chapter three.

A false spirituality is someone who claims to walk with God but doesn't watch their mouth. So, what is true spirituality? James tells us in v. 27. First, it's people who "visit orphans and widows in their affliction."

The neediest and most vulnerable people in the early church were orphans and widows. Why? Because they didn't have welfare programs or life insurance policies. If family or friends didn't take them in, they would most likely die. The broader idea of v. 27 is that true believers in Jesus will serve people who are in need. We have been saved to serve!

Jesus led with a servant's towel, not a scepter. He not only modeled servanthood to His disciples, but He also taught it to them. Shortly before going to the cross, He said, "If I then, your Lord and Teacher, have washed your feet, you also ought to wash one another's feet." Going to church and reading your Bible are good, but are you serving those in need? James says this is a "pure and undefiled" religion before God.

James ends the chapter with another mark of true spirituality. It's the person who remains "unstained from the world." In other words, someone who remains holy in an unholy world. This kind of faith is only possible in the power of Christ and through the constant use of God's Word.

Day 10

Day 10 Personal Reflection

How are you helping the poor and needy? Who do you need to pull out the "servant's towel" for this week?

Partiality
James 2:1-13

¹My brothers, show no partiality as you hold the faith in our Lord Jesus Christ, the Lord of glory. ²For if a man wearing a gold ring and fine clothing comes into your assembly, and a poor man in shabby clothing also comes in, ³and if you pay attention to the one who wears the fine clothing and say, "You sit here in a good place," while you say to the poor man, "You stand over there," or, "Sit down at my feet," ⁴have you not then made distinctions among yourselves and become judges with evil thoughts? ⁵Listen, my beloved brothers, has not God chosen those who are poor in the world to be rich in faith and heirs of the kingdom, which he has promised to those who love him? ⁶But you have dishonored the poor man. Are not the rich the ones who oppress you, and the ones who drag you into court? ⁷Are they not the ones who blaspheme the honorable name by which you were called? ⁸If you really fulfill the royal law according to the Scripture, "You shall love your neighbor as yourself," you are doing well. ⁹But if you show partiality, you are committing sin and are convicted by the law as transgressors. ¹⁰For whoever keeps the whole law but fails in one point has become guilty of all of it. ¹¹For he who said, "Do not commit adultery," also said, "Do not murder." If you do not commit adultery but do murder, you have become a transgressor of the law. ¹²So speak and so act as those who are to be judged under the law of liberty. ¹³For judgment is without mercy to one who has shown no mercy. Mercy triumphs over judgment.

Day 11

¹My brothers, show no partiality as you hold the faith in our Lord Jesus Christ, the Lord of glory. ²For if a man wearing a gold ring and fine clothing comes into your assembly, and a poor man in shabby clothing also comes in, ³and if you pay attention to the one who wears the fine clothing and say, "You sit here in a good place," while you say to the poor man, "You stand over there," or, "Sit down at my feet," ⁴have you not then made distinctions among yourselves and become judges with evil thoughts?
James 2:1-4

How we treat people reveals a lot about our relationship (or lack of relationship) with God. This is the theme of James 2. In v. 1, James states the Biblical principle. In vs. 2-3, he gives a very real example. And in v. 4, he shares why a violation of this Biblical principle is a problem.

James opens the chapter by clearly laying out the Biblical principle . . . followers of Christ should "show no partiality." The gospel is not compatible with showing favoritism. Galatians 3:28 says, "There is neither Jew

> *Every life has value because every human is created in the image of God.*

nor Greek, there is neither slave nor free, there is no male and female, for you are all one in Christ Jesus."

James gives as an example a wealthy man and a poor man coming to church. If you pay special attention to the wealthy man and give him the best place to sit and show disdain for the poor man and give him the worst seat, then you have shown partiality. You have indicated the rich man has more value than the poor man.

This is a clear violation of God's love. 1 Samuel 16:7b says: "For the Lord sees not as man sees: man looks on the outward appearance, but the Lord looks on the heart." The measure of a man or woman isn't the color of their skin, their gender, or their socio-economic status, according to Scripture.

Every life has value because every human is created in the image of God. And, every life has value because Jesus died on the cross for all of mankind. If we don't get that, and we don't live that, we have made distinctions and "become judges." In other words, we have judged some people to be of more value than others. And James goes so far as to call that "evil."

It's easy to assume we don't show favoritism. But, let's do some soul-searching. Can we honestly say we would embrace a person with the stench of alcohol and dirty clothing just as much as we would a clean-cut middle-aged person? Would we be comfortable sharing a meal with a homeless person living on the street? What a challenging portion of Scripture to take to heart.

Day 11

Day 11 Personal Reflection

How do you struggle with showing partiality? How do you sometimes struggle with a judgmental spirit?

_____

_____

_____

_____

_____

_____

_____

_____

_____

_____

_____

_____

_____

Day 12

⁵Listen, my beloved brothers, has not God chosen those who are poor in the world to be rich in faith and heirs of the kingdom, which he has promised to those who love him? ⁶But you have dishonored the poor man. Are not the rich the ones who oppress you, and the ones who drag you into court? ⁷Are they not the ones who blaspheme the honorable name by which you were called?
James 2:5-7

In describing the gospel, the Bible uses several paradoxes: The first shall be last, and the last shall be first. Save your life and you will lose it, lose your life and you will find it, just to mention a few. In v. 5, we have a paradox: It is the poor who are rich. Of course, this has nothing to do with material possessions but everything to do with eternity.

Many of the readers of James' letter would have been on the lower end of the socioeconomic ladder. In some cases, this was as a result of religious persecution. The kingdom of God is an "upside-down" kingdom. It contrasts the values of this world. It is the poor who understand their

> The kingdom of God is an "upside-down" kingdom. It contrasts the values of this world.

need for the Savior. The rich oftentimes think they have all they need.

Now, the gospel is for the rich and the poor. But one must come "poor in spirit" to enter the kingdom (Matthew 5:3). The criteria for the kingdom is not how much you have or don't have. According to the end of v. 5, it is for those who love Him. Jesus said it was harder for the rich to enter the kingdom (Matthew 19:23) because the love of stuff can supersede the love of the Savior. Remember, we cannot love both God and money.

James spends the first half of chapter 2 focusing on favoritism. Specifically, the well-off being treated better in worship gatherings than the poor. James reminds believers it is the rich who "oppress you," "drag you into court," and "blaspheme the honorable name by which you were called." He presents a practical argument . . . Why would you treat them better than the ones who have not persecuted you?

Are we so eager to be accepted by the world that we will tolerate poor treatment of the poor and disregard for our God? Do we care so much for the approval of the wealthy and influential, that we would compromise our faith and dishonor the One we are called to love? Let us remember that it is the poor, in the Gospels, that Jesus seems to take extra care and concern for.

Day 12

Day 12 Personal Reflection

In what ways are you tempted to let the opinions of the wealthy and influential matter too much to you? How could you unconditionally love the poor and needy?

Day 13

⁸If you really fulfill the royal law according to the Scripture, "You shall love your neighbor as yourself," you are doing well. ⁹But if you show partiality, you are committing sin and are convicted by the law as transgressors.
James 2:8-9

The recipients of James' letter were primarily Jewish. They would have had a good grasp of the Old Testament law. As James continued to argue against showing favoritism, he appealed to the royal law of Scripture (v. 8). The Old Covenant Law, according to Leviticus 19:18, says, "You shall not take vengeance or bear a grudge against the sons of your own people, but you shall love your neighbor as yourself: I am the Lord."

While New Covenant believers were no longer bound by the Old Covenant, any moral teachings from The Law, repeated by Jesus and other New Testament authors, were still binding for the believers. It was Jesus who said all of the Law could be summarized by one ultimate law, the law of love.

> Love God and love others. There is no greater law.

Beyond Sunday

In Mark 12:30-31, Jesus said, "'And you shall love the Lord your God with all your heart and with all your soul and with all your mind and with all your strength' . . . 'You shall love your neighbor as yourself.' There is no other commandment greater than these." Love God and love others. There is no greater law.

James says in v. 9 that to show partiality is a sin because it violates the law of love. It does not reflect a love of God or others. It does not show a love for God, because it despises that which matters deeply to God. We are to love what God loves. God loves the poor and needy. And favoritism, or partiality, certainly does not reflect a love toward others.

Notice in v. 8, James calls the law of love, a *royal* love. Royal carries the idea of sovereign or supreme. There is no greater law than to love. But it may also carry the idea of a law that reflects the King, King Jesus. Jesus gave the simple call to being His disciple: "Follow me" (Matthew 4:19). Are we following Jesus in the royal law? Does our love know no partiality?

Day 13

Day 13 Personal Reflection

How does your love reflect the love of Jesus?
Who are you struggling to show love to?

Day 14

¹⁰For whoever keeps the whole law but fails in one point has become guilty of all of it. ¹¹For he who said, "Do not commit adultery," also said, "Do not murder." If you do not commit adultery but do murder, you have become a transgressor of the law.
James 2:10-11

James continues to appeal to the Old Testament Law that the Jewish readers would have studied. He quotes directly from the Ten Commandments (Exodus 20). He gives, as examples, two extreme commandments: "Do not commit adultery" and "Do not murder."

Being a transgressor of either of these laws in the Old Testament was punishable by death. Perhaps James wanted to reveal just how big of a deal violating the law of love, specifically favoritism, was in the eyes of God.

> Jesus was able to love deeply those far from God without compromising their need for holiness.

Can you imagine being guilty of murder, standing in front of a judge, saying, "Yeah, but I didn't commit adultery." What good would that do? They would still be pronounced guilty. That is the point James is making. You can't claim to love in some ways but not in other ways. We are to love in all ways. More specifically to the context, we are to love all people the same way.

The specific challenge James is giving is to not show partiality in who you treat lovingly based on socio-economic background. But let's broaden the application a bit. Are there people we don't love like we should based on the color of their skin? Do we treat one gender better than another? Do we show love to a same-sex couple, or do we only love those who share our Biblical worldview?

It's clear when you read the Gospels, Jesus went out of His way to love those who were rejected by the religious establishment. Jesus was able to love deeply those far from God without compromising their need for holiness. He gave us the ultimate example of what it looks like to balance love and truth. Could the same be said of us?

The religious leaders of the day failed to show the people how to love the unbeliever. This was one of the reasons Jesus came down hard on them. They were religious, yet they were far from God and didn't even realize it. Their lives did not reflect the royal law of love. Instead, they were marked by spiritual pride and self-righteousness. May we strive to love like Jesus while still holding on to the truth.

Day 14

Day 14 Personal Reflection

How well are you balancing truth and love?
How well are you loving those far from God?

Day 15

¹²So speak and so act as those who are to be judged under the law of liberty. ¹³For judgment is without mercy to one who has shown no mercy. Mercy triumphs over judgment.
James 2:12-13

God's mercy *in* us should overflow *out* of us. The "law of liberty" (v. 12) is the truth of the gospel that we have been set free from sin, because of God's mercy, through the work of Jesus Christ, His death, and His resurrection. This incredible mercy should cause us to be the most mercy-filled people on the planet.

And yet, James concludes this section on favoritism by reminding the believers that not showing equal love to the poor will be judged by the Father. We will give an account of our speech and our actions. We may have been set free from the penalty of sin, but we still will answer for how we live and what we say. Do our lives reflect a loving and merciful spirit toward the poor and needy?

> We may have been set free from the penalty of sin, but we still will answer for how we live and what we say.

According to v. 13, we will be

shown no mercy when we have shown no mercy. Jesus taught about this in a parable in Matthew 18. A servant owed a large sum of money to the king. When the servant couldn't pay it, he was ordered to be sold into slavery along with his family. The servant begged for mercy and the king relented. Not only did the king not sell him, but he also forgave the man's large debt.

And yet, sometime later, this same servant went to a man who owed him a small amount of money. When the man begged for mercy, he was shown none. In fact, he had the man thrown into prison. When the king heard of this, he summoned the servant and said to him, "You wicked servant! I forgave you all that debt because you pleaded with me. And should not you have had mercy on your fellow servant, as I had mercy on you" (Matthew 18:33)?

The man received judgment for his lack of mercy. He was imprisoned until he could pay back the debt he owed. We should give mercy because of the mercy shown to us. God will judge the merciless. I love the way James ends, "Mercy triumphs over judgment" (v. 13). May we spend less time judging others and more time showing mercy. For this is the way of Jesus.

Can you imagine being guilty of murder, standing in front of a judge, saying, "Yeah, but I didn't commit adultery." What good would that do? They would still be pronounced guilty. That is the point James is making. You can't claim to love in

Day 15

Day 15 Personal Reflection

*Would others consider you a person of mercy?
Who in your life needs to be shown mercy and love?*

Faith and Works
James 2:14-26

14What good is it, my brothers, if someone says he has faith but does not have works? Can that faith save him? 15If a brother or sister is poorly clothed and lacking in daily food, 16and one of you says to them, "Go in peace, be warmed and filled," without giving them the things needed for the body, what good is that? 17So also faith by itself, if it does not have works, is dead. 18But someone will say, "You have faith and I have works." Show me your faith apart from your works, and I will show you my faith by my works. 19You believe that God is one; you do well. Even the demons believe—and shudder! 20Do you want to be shown, you foolish person, that faith apart from works is useless? 21Was not Abraham our father justified by works when he offered up his son Isaac on the altar? 22You see that faith was active along with his works, and faith was completed by his works; 23and the Scripture was fulfilled that says, "Abraham believed God, and it was counted to him as righteousness"—and he was called a friend of God. 24You see that a person is justified by works and not by faith alone. 25And in the same way was not also Rahab the prostitute justified by works when she received the messengers and sent them out by another way? ²⁶For as the body apart from the spirit is dead, so also faith apart from works is dead.

Day 16

¹⁴What good is it, my brothers, if someone says he has faith but does not have works? Can that faith save him?
James 2:14

Have you ever had someone jokingly say to you, "What good are you?" after you mess something up? James uses a similar phrase in v. 14, "What good is it?" What is the "it" James is talking about?

It's a faith that has no works to show for it. It's pointless. It accomplishes nothing. In other words, what good is it? There are two extremes when it comes to the subject of salvation. The first extreme is easy belief-ism. Just "say a prayer" and you're saved, even if there is no true inward repentance. The second extreme is a work-based religion without a true relationship.

At first glance, this section of Scripture may seem like a contradiction to the gospel. At the heart of Christianity is the belief that humans cannot save themselves by good works. Ephesians 2:8-9 says, "For by grace you have been saved through faith. And this is not your own doing; it is the gift of God, not a

> We are not saved by good works, but we are saved for good works.

result of works, so that no one may boast."

Easy belief-ism isn't the gospel because saving faith involves turning from self and handing over the reins of leadership to Jesus. A works-based religion isn't the gospel because it trusts in our human works instead of the saving work of Christ, His death, and resurrection.

James is writing to those who have already embraced the gospel by faith in Christ alone. He is not describing the gospel as Paul was in the book of Romans. He is challenging the believers on what the result of the gospel should be in our lives, which is good works.

Think of it this way, we are not saved by good works, but we are saved for good works. Ephesians 2:8-9 reveals how we are saved. It's in Ephesians v. 10 that we see part of the reason why we were saved: "For we are his workmanship, created in Christ Jesus for good works, which God prepared beforehand, that we should walk in them."

James asked in v. 14, "Can that faith save him?" What faith? The kind that does not produce good works. Is there evidence of salvation in your life? Good works produced by faith are the evidence.

Day 16

Day 16 Personal Reflection

What evidence would you present for your salvation? In what ways are you demonstrating you are God's "workmanship?"

Day 17

^{15}If a brother or sister is poorly clothed and lacking in daily food, ^{16}and one of you says to them, "Go in peace, be warmed and filled," without giving them the things needed for the body, what good is that? ^{17}So also faith by itself, if it does not have works, is dead.
James 2:14

In v. 14, James makes the argument that if a person's life isn't marked by good works, it's evidence the person has not truly attained saving faith. In vs. 15-16, he gives an example of what kind of good works should mark the life of a Christ follower.

If a person you know "is poorly clothed and lacking in daily food" (v. 15) and you wish them well "without giving them the things needed for the body" (v. 16), then, according to the end of v. 16, "what good is that?"

Talk is cheap. Anyone can say, "Go in peace, be warmed and filled." There is no cost to that. There is no sacrifice in that. Good work isn't about talk, it's about action. The problem some have with believers is, oftentimes, it appears we talk the talk

> Evidence of true faith is that we will love the beaten and the bloodied as Jesus does.

Beyond Sunday

but don't walk the walk. Helping the hurting is evidence of genuine faith.

James is not one to hold back. His words are sometimes blunt. That's exactly what we see in v. 17. He says our faith is dead if we don't have the kind of faith that helps those who are in need. This role is not just for pastors and missionaries. Every believer is called to follow in the ways of Jesus. And it's impossible to read the Gospels and not see that Jesus went to the poor and hurting.

Perhaps James remembered the story his brother Jesus told when writing these words. It's the parable of the Good Samaritan (Luke 10:25-37). When two different religious people came across a man badly beaten and bleeding, they walked on the other side and did nothing.

But a Samaritan, a person despised by the Jewish religious establishment, took pity on the man, taking care of him at great personal cost. This story was told after Jesus had been asked, "And who is my neighbor?" Through the story, Jesus said your neighbor is anyone you come in contact with who is in need of love and mercy.

Evidence of true faith is that we will love the beaten and the bloodied as Jesus does. And even at great personal cost, we will help meet the needs of those God has placed in our path. Who has God placed in your path? How will you demonstrate a faith that produces good works?

Day 17

Day 17 Personal Reflection

Is there anyone "beaten and bloodied" in your path right now? How could you serve them?

Day 18

> [18]*But someone will say, "You have faith and I have works." Show me your faith apart from your works, and I will show you my faith by my works.* [19]*You believe that God is one; you do well. Even the demons believe—and shudder!*
> **James 2:18-19**

James begins v. 18 with an imaginary objector to what he has written about in this section on faith and works. The objector's argument is," You have faith and I have works." It's an argument that you can have one without the other. But James states real faith will always include good works ("I will show you my faith *by* my works").

A deedless faith is a useless faith. To borrow from the Frank Sinatra song, "You can't have one without the other."[1] James brings his point home in a shocking way. He says if their faith doesn't lead to Christlike good works, then their faith is no better than the demons! As you've probably already noticed, James is not one to "pull punches."

James begins with a statement every religious Jew would recite daily, called the *Shema*. It comes from Deuteronomy 6:4:

> A deedless faith is a useless faith.

Beyond Sunday

"Hear, O Israel: The Lord our God, the Lord is one." In a polytheistic world, the Jewish people believed in only one God (existing in three persons- Father, Son, and Holy Spirit). Which is very good theology.

But guess what? Hell will be filled with people who have good theology. Even the demons have good theology. They also believe there is only one God. They even have a healthy fear of God. They "shudder" (v. 19) when they think of God. The point is, neither intellectual understanding nor emotionalism is enough to save.

Deuteronomy 6:5-6 reveals it's more than just believing in who God is: "You shall love
the Lord your God with all your heart and with all your soul and with all your might. And these words that I command you today shall be on your heart." Our hearts must fall in love with who God is. He can't just have our heads, He must have our hearts.

Once God truly has our hearts, the result will be gospel-centered works fueled by a love for the Father. It was the Apostle Paul who said, "For Christ's love compels us" (2 Corinthians 5:14a, NIV). The question is today, "Do I love the Lord our God with all of my heart, with all of my soul, and with all of my might?"

Day 18

Day 18 Personal Reflection

In what ways are you loving God with all of your being? What is a threat to your growing love for God?

Day 19

²⁰Do you want to be shown, you foolish person, that faith apart from works is useless? ²¹Was not Abraham our father justified by works when he offered up his son Isaac on the altar? ²²You see that faith was active along with his works, and faith was completed by his works; ²³and the Scripture was fulfilled that says, "Abraham believed God, and it was counted to him as righteousness" —and he was called a friend of God.
James 2:20-23

James begins to wrap up his argument that a deedless faith is a useless faith by giving two examples from the Old Testament. The Jewish father, Abraham, and the foreign prostitute, Rahab. In today's verses, the focus is on Abraham, the one most associated with faith for Jewish believers.

James will argue in these verses Abraham's life was marked by both faith and actions. He begins with the phrase "you foolish person" (v. 20). This seems harsh, but the Greek word used here carries the idea of "empty or hollow." If there's no outward fruit in your faith, then you have an empty faith that is not pro-

> What better description to have for our lives, that we are friends with God!

Beyond Sunday

ducing anything.

It's important to remember it's not perfect fruit. Abraham made his fair share of mistakes. He lied twice, claiming his wife was his sister, out of fear for his life (Genesis 12 and 20). He gave into Sarah's demands to try and have the promised child through their servant Hagar. There were times when Abraham was faithless, but God remained faithful to him.

The ultimate example of Abraham's faith leading to action was his willingness to sacrifice his precious son Isaac (Genesis 22). Imagine being willing to take the life of the son you waited nearly a century to have. Of course, God would not require Isaac's life, but Abraham demonstrated that there was no relationship above his relationship with God. Can each of us say that as well?

In Genesis 12, God promised Abraham that he would be the father of a great nation (Israel) that God would make as His specially chosen people. Abraham was quite old when God made the promise! And yet Abraham believed it, and it was "counted to him as righteousness." Do we believe that God can do what seems impossible?

And, don't miss how v. 23 ends, ". . . he was called a friend of God." What better description to have for our lives than that of we are friends with God?! Is God your highest priority? Your most pursued relationship?

Day 19

Day 19 Personal Reflection

What gets in the way of pursuing God? What, in your life, needs to be sacrificed to God?

Day 20

^{24}You see that a person is justified by works and not by faith alone. ^{25}And in the same way was not also Rahab the prostitute justified by works when she received the messengers and sent them out by another way? ^{26}For as the body apart from the spirit is dead, so also faith apart from works is dead.
James 2:24-26

While we are saved by faith in Christ alone, it is our works that are the evidence that our faith is genuine. That has been James' challenge in this chapter. And he ends the topic by mentioning an unlikely hero of faith: a woman named Rahab.

While Abraham was a Jewish man, Rahab was a Gentile woman. Abraham was a patriarch, and Rahab was a prostitute. He was wealthy, she was poor. Yet, God used this scandalous woman to help the Israelites enter the promised land. What a reminder to each of us that God doesn't need great talent or charisma. He is looking for obedient faith.

Never discount what God can do in your life. Paul was a man who persecuted the church, perhaps even to the point of death. But God changed him, and he

> *Never discount what God can do in your life.*

became the most influential missionary of the early church. He wrote more books of the Bible than anyone else. It was Paul who wrote, "But God chose what is foolish in the world to shame the wise; God chose what is weak in the world to shame the strong" (1 Corinthians 1:27).

How did Rahab help the Jews? According to Joshua 2, Jewish spies came across Rahab in the city of Jericho. The Jericho police were trying to track down the spies, and it was Rahab who offered them cover in her home. She risked her life because, apparently, she had come to faith in God. That's the kind of thing that happens when one comes to a saving knowledge of the Savior. They are willing to risk everything for God and His kingdom.

James closes out Chapter 2 with a comparison: "For as the body apart from the spirit is dead, so also faith apart from works is dead." Obviously, if your spirit leaves your body, you are dead! Maybe not in the movies but definitely in real life! So also, if a person claims to have faith in Christ but there is no evidence of spiritual fruit ("works") in his life, he is a "dead man walking."

As mentioned before, a deedless faith is a useless faith. Let's not waste our lives. Let's give ourselves to kingdom work, in light of Jesus' work on our behalf, His death and resurrection.

Day 20

Day 20 Personal Reflection

How are you demonstrating a true belief that God can do great things in your life? What are some tangible ways you could step out by faith?

Words
James 3:1-12

¹*Not many of you should become teachers, my brothers, for you know that we who teach will be judged with greater strictness. ²For we all stumble in many ways. And if anyone does not stumble in what he says, he is a perfect man, able also to bridle his whole body. ³If we put bits into the mouths of horses so that they obey us, we guide their whole bodies as well. ⁴Look at the ships also: though they are so large and are driven by strong winds, they are guided by a very small rudder wherever the will of the pilot directs. ⁵So also the tongue is a small member, yet it boasts of great things. How great a forest is set ablaze by such a small fire! ⁶And the tongue is a fire, a world of unrighteousness. The tongue is set among our members, staining the whole body, setting on fire the entire course of life, and set on fire by hell. ⁷For every kind of beast and bird, of reptile and sea creature, can be tamed and has been tamed by mankind, ⁸but no human being can tame the tongue. It is a restless evil, full of deadly poison. ⁹With it we bless our Lord and Father, and with it we curse people who are made in the likeness of God. ¹⁰From the same mouth come blessing and cursing. My brothers, these things ought not to be so. ¹¹Does a spring pour forth*

from the same opening both fresh and salt water? ¹²Can a fig tree, my brothers, bear olives, or a grapevine produce figs? Neither can a salt pond yield fresh water.

Day 21

¹Not many of you should become teachers, my brothers, for you know that we who teach will be judged with greater strictness. ²For we all stumble in many ways. And if anyone does not stumble in what he says, he is a perfect man, able also to bridle his whole body.
James 3:1-2

As someone who has taught God's Word for over thirty years, v. 1 is one of the most challenging verses in the Bible for me. Biblical teachers "will be judged with greater strictness." Why is that? Because teachers have an incredible influence on people's lives, for good or for bad.

Another reason is, correct doctrine is important to the Christian faith. A teacher with bad theology can lead people down an unbiblical path. That's why it's important for every believer to be a student of the Word of God. Each person needs to learn to discern what they hear, so they are not led astray by false teaching.

> Our mouth plays a role in how healthy or unhealthy our life and relationships will be.

What a teacher says matters.

Beyond Sunday

James, then, transitions to all believers. James says not to "stumble" in what we say in v. 2. And if we don't, we are "perfect." Now, we all know we won't be perfect until Jesus returns. The Greek word for "perfect" (v. 2) is *teleios* which means "complete, mature." James is saying that being wise with our words is a sign of spiritual maturity.

James then says something curious. He says, if a person doesn't stumble in what they say, that person is "able also to bridle his whole body" (v. 2). The whole body controlled by the tongue? The "whole body" in this verse probably means a person's whole being. In other words, if a Christ follower can learn to tame the tongue, this person will most likely be able to discipline and control the rest of their life.

The apostle Peter talked about the importance of what a person says. In 1 Peter 2:10, he wrote, "Whoever desires to love life and see good days, let him keep his tongue from evil and his lips from speaking deceit."

I don't know about you, but I definitely want to "love life and see good days." Our mouth plays a role in how healthy or unhealthy our lives and relationships will be. James will go on over the next ten verses presenting a compelling argument for taming the tongue. How about you? Are you wise with your words? What we say will impact how we live.

Day 21

Day 21 Personal Reflection

*How are you intentional about what you choose to say?
What is your biggest challenge when it comes to words?*

_____

_____

_____

_____

_____

_____

_____

_____

_____

_____

_____

_____

_____

_____

Day 22

³If we put bits into the mouths of horses so that they obey us, we guide their whole bodies as well. ⁴Look at the ships also: though they are so large and are driven by strong winds, they are guided by a very small rudder wherever the will of the pilot directs. ⁵So also the tongue is a small member, yet it boasts of great things.
James 3:3-5

In vs. 3-5, James teaches about the power of the tongue. He uses two analogies: horses and ships. Horses are powerful creatures. A horse can weigh anywhere from 800 to 2,000 pounds. They are able to pull up to 2,500 pounds. Horses are a half-ton of raw power. Yet, this powerful beast can be tamed by an itty-bitty horse bit, about five inches long and only weighing a few pounds. The bit literally lies on the top of the horse's tongue.

I've ridden a horse a few times. You don't realize just how big and powerful they are until you sit on one. And yet, with a little jerk on the reins, which are connected to the bit, you can move the horse in any direction you want. Just like a bit, the tongue

> The tongue is just a 2 ounce organ, yet it can change lives forever.

can move our lives in a healthy or unhealthy direction.

Cruise ships weigh approximately 220,000 tons. That's 440 million pounds! And what controls this massive piece of metal? A small metal flap called a rudder. This is the power of small things. The tongue is just a two-ounce organ, yet it can change lives forever. Proverbs 18:21 says, "Death and life are in the power of the tongue, and those who love it will eat its fruits."

In other words, King Solomon (the author of the proverb) is saying a wise person understands the power of our words and, therefore, pays very close attention to how they are using them, for good and not for evil. There is a great reward when we speak to build up instead of to tear down.

Solomon's dad, King David, also talked about the use of words. In Psalm 39:1 he said, "I
will guard my ways, that I may not sin with my tongue; I will guard my mouth with a muzzle, so long as the wicked are in my presence." How are you guarding your mouth? Your words possess the power for good or bad.

Day 22

Day 22 Personal Reflection

What could help you better guard your mouth? In what ways could you start praying for wisdom with your words?

Day 23

⁶And the tongue is a fire, a world of unrighteousness. The tongue is set among our members, staining the whole body, setting on fire the entire course of life, and set on fire by hell. ⁷For every kind of beast and bird, of reptile and sea creature, can be tamed and has been tamed by mankind, ⁸but no human being can tame the tongue. It is a restless evil, full of deadly poison.
James 3:6-8

James continues his warning of the total destruction the tongue can produce. He now moves from horses and ships to fire. The tongue can destroy like a fire that rages out of control.
James describes it as "a world of unrighteousness" (v. 6).

Perhaps when writing these verses, he was remembering the words of Solomon: "For lack of wood the fire goes out, and where there is no whisperer, quarreling ceases. As charcoal to hot embers and wood to fire, so is a quarrelsome man for kindling strife" (Proverbs 26:20-21).

A fire goes out when no wood is added to the fire, just as a person who refuses to gossip will put out dissension in a relationship. But a person who doesn't

> *An untamed tongue comes straight from hell!*

guard his mouth will only cause the fire of dissension to grow. So, do you start fires or do you put out fires with your words? The tongue has "burned down" many families, churches, and organizations.

The tongue cannot only destroy other people's lives, it can also destroy our own. James calls it "staining the whole body" (v. 6). Unrighteous talk can lead to an unrighteous life, "setting on fire the entire course of life" (v. 6). These are strong words, but that's the point. James needs the believers to understand just how potent our words can be.

And no stronger words does he use than the phrase "set on fire by hell" (v. 6). The Greek word for hell here is *Gehenna*. Gehenna was the place outside of Jerusalem where they burnt all the garbage from the city, a place of fire and filth. An untamed tongue comes straight from hell! Have you noticed how blunt James is?

James has a penchant for analogies. He gives one more in these verses . . . animals. He writes that animals can be tamed, "but no human being can tame the tongue" (v. 8). He did not say the tongue can't be tamed. He said no human can tame it. We need the power of Christ if we're ever going to have victory in this area.

In case we haven't caught the message about the tongue, he ends v. 8 with, "It is a restless evil, full of deadly poison." Sometimes in life, we need an arm around our shoulders, but other times, we need a swift kick in the pants. This is that kick in the pants. We must seek God's help in taming this wild beast known as the tongue. Are you praying regularly that God will help you guard your words?

Day 23

Day 23 Personal Reflection

Are your words reflecting heaven or hell? Who is someone you could ask to help keep you accountable with your words?

Day 24

⁹With it we bless our Lord and Father, and with it we curse people who are made in the likeness of God. ¹⁰From the same mouth come blessing and cursing. My brothers, these things ought not to be so.
James 3:9-10

"Two roads diverged . . ./and I—/ I took the one less traveled by,/ and that has made all the difference."² How fitting are the words of Robert Frost in today's passage? We have two "roads" to choose from when we speak: the road that blesses or the road that curses. When both are a part of our speech, James says, "these things ought not to be so" (v. 10).

What ought to be so is to "bless our Lord and Father" (v. 9). In the context of our words, what does it mean to bless God? The word bless in Greek is *Eulogoumen* (where we get our English word "Eulogy"). It means "saying a good word." In this context, the idea is that our words should speak well of God.

> Duplicity in our speech is an offense to God and a detriment to our Christian witness.

1 Chronicles 29:10 says, "Therefore David blessed the Lord in the presence of all the assembly. And David said: 'Blessed are

Beyond Sunday

you, O Lord, the God of Israel our father, forever and ever.'" Like David, we bless God when we praise Him to others, and we bless God when we praise Him directly.

What doesn't bless God is when, with the same mouth, "we curse people who are made in the likeness of God" (v. 9). The word curse carries the idea of "wishing evil." If you curse at someone, you are wishing them evil. James goes back to creation to remind every human is created in the image of God (Genesis 1:26).

When we curse people, whether that is literally cursing at them or cursing them by speaking unkindly to them or about them, it is like wishing evil upon God, because all of us are created in His image. If that isn't motivation to be careful with our words, I don't know what is! We can't bless God one minute and curse people, created in his image, the next minute.

Duplicity in our speech is an offense to God and a detriment to our Christian witness. It has no place in the life of a Christ follower. May our words match what we claim to believe. Let us bless God and others with the words we speak.

Day 24

Day 24 Personal Reflection

*How are you intentionally blessing God with your words?
Are there any ways your words are a curse to others?*

Day 25

[11]Does a spring pour forth from the same opening both fresh and salt water? [12]Can a fig tree, my brothers, bear olives, or a grapevine produce figs? Neither can a salt pond yield fresh water.
James 3:11-12

Horses, ships, fire, and animals. This chapter is filled with images intended to teach the readers about how one uses the tongue. James concludes his exhortation of the tongue with yet some more analogies, bodies of water, a tree, a grapevine, olives, and figs.

A body of water will not produce both fresh and salt water nor would a fig tree produce olives or a grapevine produce figs. These are obvious contradictions that would never occur. And that's what James is getting at. Followers of Jesus should never have words come out of their mouths that don't reflect the righteousness of God.

> Followers of Jesus should never have words come out of their mouths that don't reflect the righteousness of God.

Proverbs 10:11a says, "The mouth of the righteous is a fountain of life." Our words should be life-giving. And yet, all of us know there is still a struggle for our words to always match up to our faith. This side of heaven, as long as we have a sin nature, we will have to do battle with our mouths. Praise the Lord, our Father is a forgiving God.

If you struggle with your words, know that victory is possible. Because Jesus rose from the dead, you have resurrection power available to you! Memorize some Bible verses about the tongue. Find an accountability partner. Pray each day for God's help. Examine the heart, because Scripture says the words that come out of our mouths reveal what's happening in the heart.

Our words have power. Proverbs 15:4 says, "A gentle tongue is a tree of life, but perverseness in it breaks the spirit." We can be a tree of life, or we can break the spirit. We must repent of gossip. We must repent of negative, critical talk. We must repent of vulgar language. That's when growth can occur.

1 John 1:9 says, "If we confess our sins, he is faithful and just to forgive us our sins and to cleanse us from all unrighteousness." God not only forgives, but He also wants to help cleanse us from all unrighteous talk. May all of us pray the prayer of David: "Let the words of my mouth and the meditation of my hear

Day 25

Day 25 Personal Reflection

Who needs to be nourished by your words? How has this passage challenged you in regards to the tongue?

Wisdom

James 3:13-18

[13]Who is wise and understanding among you? By his good conduct let him show his works in the meekness of wisdom. [14]But if you have bitter jealousy and selfish ambition in your hearts, do not boast and be false to the truth. [15]This is not the wisdom that comes down from above, but is earthly, unspiritual, demonic. [16]For where jealousy and selfish ambition exist, there will be disorder and every vile practice. [17]But the wisdom from above is first pure, then peaceable, gentle, open to reason, full of mercy and good fruits, impartial and sincere. [18]And a harvest of righteousness is sown in peace by those who make peace.

Day 26

¹³Who is wise and understanding among you?
By his good conduct let him show his works
in the meekness of wisdom.
James 3:13

James begins this section on wisdom with a question of who is wise. He isn't asking for a show of hands, but if he was, most of us would want our hands to go up. But James says the answer to whether or not we are wise is evidenced by our conduct. Wisdom will produce "good conduct."

James hit on conduct in the last chapter. A genuine faith will produce good conduct. But before we look at good conduct, let's define wisdom. Wisdom is knowledge, lived out, effectively. A person can have a lot of knowledge but not be wise. This person is a smart fool.

A wise person not only knows how to apply Biblical truth, but he lives it. He knows how to take the truths of the Word and apply those truths at home, at work, and in the daily decisions of life. As a result, a wise person is a blessing to those around

> A person can have a lot of knowledge but not be wise. This person is a smart fool.

them.

It goes without saying, but a person can only have wisdom when they have regularly studied God's Word. You can't apply what you don't know. The Psalmist wrote, "I have stored up your word in my heart, that I might not sin against you" (Psalm 119:11). We need the Word for wisdom.

A truly wise person doesn't just choose to do the right thing. They do so "in the meekness of wisdom." The word meekness is used to describe a mighty horse that has been brought under control. It's essentially "strength under control." It does not boast or brag. It does not seek attention. Meekness isn't weakness; meekness is kingdom greatness!

We see from these verses that wisdom involves both action ("good conduct") and attitude ("meekness"). A follower of Christ lives out God's Word in the day-to-day of life while doing so with a humble and gentle spirit. Does that describe your life? Are you living out the wisdom of the Word? Are you "meek and mild" like the Savior?

Day 26

Day 26 Personal Reflection

How are you doing with meekness in your life?
How do you need to grow in wisdom?

_____

_____

_____

_____

_____

_____

_____

_____

_____

_____

_____

_____

_____

Day 27

^{14}But if you have bitter jealousy and selfish ambition in your hearts, do not boast and be false to the truth. ^{15}This is not the wisdom that comes down from above, but is earthly, unspiritual, demonic.
James 3:14-15

In today's verses, James shares the opposite of godly wisdom. It's "bitter jealousy and selfish ambition" (v. 14). Our actions are a reflection of the heart. Ungodly behavior begins with ungodly thoughts. Bitter jealousy can lead to the destruction of many lives.

A jealous person cannot celebrate the success of others, and it leads to a bitter heart. Proverbs 14:30 (NLT) says, "A peaceful heart leads to a healthy body; jealousy is like cancer in the bones." Jealousy destroys the heart. And it's fueled by selfish ambition. The person who lives to exalt himself will always struggle with a jealous spirit, because he can't stand others being above him. What a horrible way to live!

James also says the opposite of a person with godly wisdom is a person who will "boast" and be "false to the truth." A person who lives to exalt himself will

> Our actions are a reflection of the heart.

always struggle with boasting because he will want people to think well of him. Even as believers, we have to be careful of the "humble brag," which is coming across as humble but really wanting to impress.

A selfish, boasting person prone to jealousy is living "false to the truth," because the truth of God's Word has called us to a selfless, humble life. Having said that, we all are going to wrestle with pride until Christ takes us home to heaven. We have to be on guard for this because pride can destroy our relationships.

In Matthew 23:11-12, Jesus taught the following: "The greatest among you shall be your servant. Whoever exalts himself will be humbled, and whoever humbles himself will be exalted." Jesus defined greatness far differently from how the world does. We must ask ourselves: "Whose kingdom am I trying to build?"

This is no small matter. Look how strongly James words things. He says when a person lives to exalt himself, it is "earthly, unspiritual, demonic" (v. 15). It doesn't take a rocket scientist to realize you do not want to be described that way. James is serious about selfish pride. It must be addressed. Has pride impacted your life and relationships? What areas of selfishness or jealousy need to be addressed?

Day 27

Day 27 Personal Reflection

In what ways are you struggling with exalting self? What areas of jealousy or selfishness do you need to bring to the Father?

Day 28

¹⁶For where jealousy and selfish ambition exist, there will be disorder and every vile practice.
James 3:16

In v. 16, James continues the discussion on jealousy and selfish ambition. He focuses, in this verse, on two consequences that jealousy and selfishness will bring into a person's life and relationships. It's important to remember there are consequences to our actions.

It's been said, "Sow a thought and you reap an action; sow an act and you reap a habit; sow a habit and you reap a character; sow a character and you reap a destiny." In James 1, the writer talked about Satan's goal to gradually lead us to destruction as we give into sin. We must realize there is a price to pay if we choose the wisdom of the world instead of the wisdom of God. James tells us in verse 16, the price will be "disorder and every vile practice." The Greek word for disorder is *Akatastasia*. It means "instability or confusion." James also used the word in James 1:8 when describing a person who isn't seeking the wisdom of God. James

> Contentment belongs to a person who has learned to find joy and peace with what they have.

says, "he is a double-minded man, unstable [*Akatastasia*] in all his ways."

Remember the context is godly wisdom versus worldly wisdom. When a person doesn't address their jealous and selfish spirit, they will never truly have a stable relationship with God or with others. And as those relationships deteriorate, it can lead to even more sinfulness ("every vile practice").

The Apostle Paul said in 1 Timothy 6:6-7, "But godliness with contentment is great gain, for we brought nothing into the world, and we cannot take anything out of the world." Content means enough. Contentment belongs to a person who has learned to find joy and peace in what they have.

Paul says more stuff can't bring contentment, because you can't take it with you anyway! Finding joy in Christ is the only cure. Letting go of self and handing over the reins to the Savior is what leads to a humble, selfless life. That's godly wisdom. It is of "great gain" as Paul said. Worldly wisdom only leads to an unstable life.

Day 28

Day 28 Personal Reflection

Is there a person you are jealous or envious of? Is there anything the Holy Spirit is leading you to bring to the foot of the cross?

Day 29

[17]But the wisdom from above is first pure, then peaceable, gentle, open to reason, full of mercy and good fruits, impartial and sincere.
James 3:17

In this section on godly wisdom versus worldly wisdom, James starts with godly wisdom (v. 13), then focuses on worldly wisdom (vs. 14-16), and ends the chapter again looking at godly wisdom (vs. 17-18). In today's verse, James gives eight characteristics of a person who is pursuing godly wisdom.

The first characteristic mentioned is purity. It says "first pure." The "first" carries the idea that this characteristic is the most important of all of them. Godly wisdom makes a person pure in heart, and out of that purity, all the other qualities flow.

It's hard to keep a pure heart in an impure world. That's why we need to come to the Bible every day for wisdom. Psalm 19:8b says, "The commandment of the Lord is pure, enlightening the eyes." Exposing ourselves to the pure Word of God will produce a pure heart which leads to "enlightening the eyes." Purity of heart leads to clarity of sight.

> *Purity of heart leads to clarity of sight.*

Beyond Sunday

A pure person will become a peaceful person. The reason they have peaceful relationships is they are gentle with those around them. Do you see how these qualities build on each other? A gentle person will be "open to reason." This is a person who isn't "set in his ways" but is open to learning, growing, and seeing things from another person's perspective. What wisdom indeed!

When we are open to seeing things from another person's perspective, it makes us much more merciful. These kinds of qualities will lead to "good fruits" in our lives and relationships. It will help us to love people impartially and with a sincere heart.

When I look at these eight characteristics, I can't help but yearn for our world to be filled with more people like this. There is so much hate and division in our world that reading these verses fills me with such a hope for heaven. Let's strive to live these characteristics of wisdom in our world today. Let our light shine in the darkness because our world desperately needs it.

Day 29

Day 29 Personal Reflection

Which of the eight characteristics of godly wisdom do you most often see exhibited in your life? Which characteristics do you need to pray for?

Day 30

¹⁸And a harvest of righteousness is sown in peace by those who make peace.
James 3:18

James tells us what godly wisdom looks like in v. 17. And now in v. 18 he tells us what the reward will be when we pursue godly wisdom in our lives. The reward is "a harvest of righteousness" and "peace."

Let's consider righteousness first. Righteousness can simply be defined as "living in a right way." It's living right before God, and it's doing the right thing by others. Theologically, it means to be declared right before God. This is not a result of our own doing. It is only made possible because of Jesus' righteous works, His death, and resurrection. We are declared righteous (justified) when we place our faith in the work of Christ on our behalf.

Once we enter into this relationship with God, we become at peace with God. Peace with God leads to inner peace, which then leads to peace with others. A life of peace and righteousness is rooted in our relationship

> *Wisdom is found in a walk with God and time in His Word.*

Beyond Sunday

with God, not through our own human efforts.

There is no way to avoid worldly wisdom (vs. 14-16) unless we have a daily personal walk with God. We become like the people we spend time with. That's why the Bible says, "Bad company corrupts good character" (1 Corinthians 15:33). But it's true in reverse as well; good company grows good character. Wisdom is found in a walk with God and time in His Word.

We also grow in wisdom when we ask God for it in prayer. Remember James 1:5? "If any of you lacks wisdom, let him ask God, who gives generously to all without reproach, and it will be given him." Walk with God through His Word and ask for it in prayer. Repent of jealousy and selfish ambition. These are the steps James says to take to be a man or woman of wisdom.

Let's close this chapter with a prayer: "And it is my prayer that your love may abound more and more, with knowledge and all discernment, so that you may approve what is excellent, and so be pure and blameless for the day of Christ, filled with the fruit of righteousness that
comes through Jesus Christ, to the glory and praise of God" (Philippians 1:9-11). Amen.

Day 30

Day 30 Personal Reflection

Which relationships, in your life, are not marked by peace? What steps could you take to pursue peace?

Worldliness
James 4:1-12

¹*What causes quarrels and what causes fights among you? Is it not this, that your passions are at war within you? ²You desire and do not have, so you murder. You covet and cannot obtain, so you fight and quarrel. You do not have, because you do not ask. ³You ask and do not receive, because you ask wrongly, to spend it on your passions. ⁴You adulterous people! Do you not know that friendship with the world is enmity with God? Therefore whoever wishes to be a friend of the world makes himself an enemy of God. ⁵Or do you suppose it is to no purpose that the Scripture says, "He yearns jealously over the spirit that he has made to dwell in us"? ⁶But he gives more grace. Therefore it says, "God opposes the proud but gives grace to the humble." ⁷Submit yourselves therefore to God. Resist the devil, and he will flee from you. ⁸Draw near to God, and he will draw near to you. Cleanse your hands, you sinners, and purify your hearts, you double-minded. ⁹Be wretched and mourn and weep. Let your laughter be turned to mourning and your joy to gloom. ¹⁰Humble yourselves before the Lord, and he will exalt you. ¹¹Do not speak evil against one another, brothers. The one who speaks against a brother or judges his brother,*

speaks evil against the law and judges the law. But if you judge the law, you are not a doer of the law but a judge. ¹²*There is only one lawgiver and judge, he who is able to save and to destroy. But who are you to judge your neighbor?*

Day 31

¹What causes quarrels and what causes fights among you? Is it not this, that your passions are at war within you? ²You desire and do not have, so you murder. You covet and cannot obtain, so you fight and quarrel. You do not have, because you do not ask. ³You ask and do not receive, because you ask wrongly, to spend it on your passions.
James 4:1-3

James is a fan of using rhetorical questions. In fact, I counted at least twenty of them in the book. He starts chapter 4 with one. "What causes quarrels and what causes fights among you?" He's actually going to answer the question with another rhetorical question. But, before we look at that, notice he says, "among you." The "you" are the Jewish Christians. It's not just the unsaved who fight. Christians struggle with strife as well.

But what causes conflicts among even believers? It's the "passions" that "are at war within you." The Greek word for passions is *hedone*. It's where we get our English word "hedonism," which is the pursuit of pleasure. Now, seeking pleasure, in and of itself, is not bad. But in this context, it's the self-

> *He knows what we need and He knows when we need it.*

ish pursuit of pleasures that do not honor God.

We are bombarded in our culture with the message that seeking our own desires is what matters most. "You do you", "If it feels good, do it", "Just listen to your heart." These ideas are humanism and have no place in the life of a Christ follower. In fact, James says that kind of living can lead to coveting and even murder (v. 2).

At the end of v. 2 and into v. 3, James says you fight and quarrel over the things you don't have because you either don't ask (v. 2c) or you ask with impure motives (v. 3). Sometimes, we don't get what we want because we aren't truly seeking God with our desires. And sometimes, we don't receive because we are praying selfishly.

God loves to give good gifts to His children (Matthew 7:11). He knows what we need, and He knows when we need it. He also knows when something isn't best for us, even when we think it is. As James wrote in 1:17: "Every good gift and every perfect gift is from above."

What a challenging passage of Scripture. Are we quarreling with others? Are our motives pure and holy? Am I seeking God's will, or my own, when I pray? These are hard but important questions to wrestle through with God.

Day 31

Day 31 Personal Reflection

In what ways are you struggling with pure motives? How are you wrestling with yielding to God's will?

Day 32

⁴You adulterous people! Do you not know that friendship with the world is enmity with God? Therefore whoever wishes to be a friend of the world makes himself an enemy of God. ⁵Or do you suppose it is to no purpose that the Scripture says, "He yearns jealously over the spirit that he has made to dwell in us"?
James 4:4-5

One thing you can't accuse James of is being a people pleaser! He says what needs to be said, whether people like it or not. Much like his brother and Savior, Jesus, James speaks the truth in love, but he doesn't hold back. He begins with these words to the believers, "You adulterous people!" Wow, harsh. But, sometimes, that's what it takes to get through to people.

Perhaps we need the same challenge. Are we adulterous? Are we trying so hard to have "friendship with the world" (v. 4) that it's hindering our intimacy with the Father? James says you can't have it both ways. If we choose "to be a friend of the world" it's like we are "an ene-

> *The world's values and God's values are not the same. Choose this day whom you will serve!*

my of God." The values of the world and God's values are *not* the same. Choose this day whom you will serve!

James goes on to say something that's hard to interpret, at the end of v. 5: "He yearns jealously over the spirit that he has made to dwell in us." It could mean the human spirit God has given us "yearns jealously." But, I'm not sure that fits the context here.

I believe the best interpretation is this: God is zealous that our inner being (spirit), through the help of the Holy Spirit, seeks after the things of God, not the things of the world. Jesus said in John 16:13, "When the Spirit of truth comes, he will guide you into all the truth." The Holy Spirit daily prompts us to live the truths of God's Word.

Every day, we have a choice, to listen to the Holy Spirit or to listen to our own desires. We are inundated every day with the message of the world, "Do what makes you feel good." For the life of the Christ follower, the message we need to listen to is, "Come and follow Me." Whose voice will we choose to listen to today?

Day 32

Day 32 Personal Reflection

How well are you listening to the Holy Spirit? How does it make you feel that God is jealous for you?

Day 33

⁶But he gives more grace. Therefore it says, "God opposes the proud but gives grace to the humble." ⁷Submit yourselves therefore to God. Resist the devil, and he will flee from you. ⁸Draw near to God, and he will draw near to you. Cleanse your hands, you sinners, and purify your hearts, you double-minded.

James 4:6-8

This section of Scripture has been hard-hitting. But James softens the blow in today's verses. He's exhorted strongly, but now, he encourages with a shepherd's heart. He opens this section with, "But he gives more grace" (v. 6a).

What separates Christianity from all other religions is one word: grace. Grace means to get what we don't deserve. Every other religion teaches what one must *do*. Christianity is rooted in what Jesus has *done*. But there is a roadblock to grace: pride.

> *Every other religion teaches what one must do. Christianity is rooted in what Jesus has done.*

Pride is what cast Lucifer out of heaven (Isaiah 14:12-15). Pride is what cast Adam and Eve out of the Garden of Eden (Genesis

3). Pride elevates oneself above others. It literally means "to exalt." In v. 6b, James quotes Proverbs 3:34: "God opposes the proud but gives grace to the humble."

While pride is the roadblock to God's grace, humility is the pathway. Humility means "lowly." It's the intent of serving God and others above ourselves. As C.S. Lewis put it, the humble person "will not be thinking about humility: he will not be thinking about himself at all."[3] The grace needed to overcome sin is available when we humble ourselves before God.

In vs. 7-8, we learn we do have a part to play in the pursuit of holy living. First, we must submit to God. It begins by acknowledging God's sovereignty and living under His authority. Doing so involves the second part, resisting the devil. Submitting to God involves running away from sin and Satan.

Are we running away or are we playing with fire? James tells us that if we resist the devil, he will flee from us. But it's not just running *from* something; it's running *to* something. Actually, it's running to Someone. There is protection in the presence of God. God promises to come to us as we come to Him. What a promise!

We need to submit, resist, and draw near. And we need to cleanse our hands and purify our hearts. As we draw near to God, we see areas of unholiness, and the response is to be cleansed and purified from them. In the next verse, James will tell us how that can come about. Submit, resist, draw near, be cleansed, and purified. Which step is your next stop to holiness?

Day 33

Day 33 Personal Reflection

*In what ways is it a struggle to submit to God?
How do you need to resist the devil this week?*

Day 34

⁹Be wretched and mourn and weep. Let your laughter be turned to mourning and your joy to gloom. ¹⁰Humble yourselves before the Lord, and he will exalt you.
James 4:9-10

The beauty of the gospel is that we are always just one repentant prayer away from being forgiven and back on the path of righteousness. However, we sometimes confuse remorse with repentance. Remorse is feeling sorry for what you've done and/or the consequences that come with it.

Repentance involves remorse but goes beyond it. To repent is the decision of the heart and the will to change behavior. 2 Corinthians 7:10 says, "Godly sorrow brings repentance." James does not use the word "repentance", but v. 9 is a description of what repentance looks like, "wretched...mourn...weep...gloom." This may seem confusing since Jesus came to give us an abundant life of joy (John 10:10).

That's true, of course, but in this

> *The beauty of the gospel is that we are always just one repentant prayer away from being forgiven and back on the path of righteousness.*

context, James is referring to a person who is living in unconfessed sin. King David committed adultery and murder (2 Samuel 11) and refused to repent for a year. Psalms 32 and 51 were written after he finally repented.

In these chapters, we see a sorrow that finally led to his repentance. David wrote, "The sacrifices of God are a broken spirit" (Psalm 51:17). The result when he finally repented? Joy! In Psalm 32:11, David wrote, "Be glad in the Lord, and rejoice, O righteous, and shout for joy, all you upright in heart!"

Here are six steps to think about when it comes to repenting of sin. Let's call them the "Road to Repentance." RECOGNIZE (*fully acknowledge the sin committed*); REMORSE (*feel genuine grief for the sin*); RELEASE (*officially confess the sin to God and ask for His forgiveness*); RESOLVE (*commit to a change of behavior*); RESTITUTION (*seek to right the wrong committed*); REJOICE (*praise God for His forgiveness*).

As you think about repentance in your own life, do you follow the full road to repentance? If not, which of the six do you need to consider the next time you stumble into sin? Notice how James ends this section. He comes back to the issue of humility.

Pride will keep us from fully acknowledging our sins. Prideful people think too highly of themselves. Repentance is for the humble, those who acknowledge they are in desperate need of God's grace. James ends with such a source of encouragement for the humble in v. 10: "he will exalt you." God exalts the humble!

Day 34

Day 34 Personal Reflection

Which "Road to Repentance" step did you need to hear today? How do you need to grow in humility?

Day 35

¹¹Do not speak evil against one another, brothers. The one who speaks against a brother or judges his brother, speaks evil against the law and judges the law. But if you judge the law, you are not a doer of the law but a judge. ¹²There is only one lawgiver and judge, he who is able to save and to destroy. But who are you to judge your neighbor?
James 4:11-12

There doesn't seem to be an obvious connection in these verses to the previous ones. But, one could argue, James is giving an example of worldliness that he was writing about in vs. 1-5 of this chapter. Worldly people speak "evil against one another" (v. 11).

James began this chapter by addressing disagreements or conflicts happening within the body of Christ. Nothing leads to dissension like speaking badly about people. It was also the topic James addressed in chapter 3. The mouth matters. What we say reflects where we are spiritually. When we speak badly of others, we are also judging them.

> *The mouth matters. What we say reflects where we are spiritually.*

Beyond Sunday

James doesn't mince words here. He says in the second half of v. 11., the person who speaks against others or judges others actually "speaks evil against the law and judges the law." Not good! Since James does not capitalize "law" nor include "the", he isn't referring to the Old Testament Law. He's referring to the law that governs the Christian life: love. In other words, speaking against or judging others violates the "royal law" of love.

This is no small matter to God. Psalm 101:5 says: "Whoever slanders his neighbor secretly I
will destroy. Whoever has a haughty look and an arrogant heart I will not endure." How we treat others and how we speak about others is of the utmost importance to God.

James concludes in v. 12 that only God has the right to ultimately make a judgment about a person's heart, because only God truly knows every intent of the heart. We will all stand and give an account someday. We will all stand and give an account someday; and I believe one of the things we will give an account for is how we treated others, how we loved or didn't love those around us (2 Corinthians 5:10, Matthew 12:36-37, Matthew 25:31-46).

James doesn't address it here, but there is a place for loving reproof within the body of Christ. We are to consider actions in light of God's Word. If a fellow believer is specifically violating God's Word, without repentance, then such reproof is in order (Galatians 6:1). The correct action is to go to the person and not behind their back to others. How are you doing in following the "royal law" of love?

Day 35

Day 35 Personal Reflection

How do you sometimes struggle with a judgmental heart? Who do you need to speak the truth in love with?

God's Will

James 4:13-17

¹³Come now, you who say, "Today or tomorrow we will go into such and such a town and spend a year there and trade and make a profit"— ¹⁴yet you do not know what tomorrow will bring. What is your life? For you are a mist that appears for a little time and then vanishes. ¹⁵Instead you ought to say, "If the Lord wills, we will live and do this or that." ¹⁶As it is, you boast in your arrogance. All such boasting is evil. ¹⁷So whoever knows the right thing to do and fails to do it, for him it is sin.

Day 36

^{13}Come now, you who say, "Today or tomorrow we will go into such and such a town and spend a year there and trade and make a profit"—
James 4:13

James begins this section on God's will by giving a hypothetical example of individuals who go on making plans for their lives, without considering what God may want from them. The opening words "Come now" are meant to be a rebuke. A modern way of saying it would be, "Get a clue."

Remember, James is writing to believers, not unbelievers. Of course, unbelievers will do whatever they feel like doing. James, here, is rebuking believers who just assume that what they want to do is what God wants them to do. It can be a very dangerous thing to make assumptions for God.

James is not rebuking people for planning ahead. The Bible commends such behavior (Proverbs 6:6-8). It's making plans without considering what's best for the kingdom of God. When Jesus taught His disciples to pray, He included, "Your kingdom

> It can be a very dangerous thing to make assumptions for God.

come, your will be done, on earth as it is in heaven" (Matt. 6:10). Decisions need to be made with eternity in mind.

Notice the example James gives. They decided for themselves *when* ("Today or tomorrow"), *where* ("into such and such a town"), *how long* ("spend a year there"), *what* ("trade"), and *why* ("make a profit"). Have you sometimes been guilty of making when, where, how long, what, and why decisions without seeking God? I must admit, I have. We must inquire of the Lord, the questions for our lives!

Like David, our hearts should sing, "I delight to do your will, O my God; your law is within my heart" (Psalm 40:8). Do we delight in our own plans, or do we delight in discovering God's plans? Oftentimes, when we delight in Him, our plans become His plans (or vice versa). Psalm 37:4 says, "Delight yourself in the Lord, and he will give you the desires of your heart."

There is a connection between time in God's Word and discovering God's will. We learn about the heart and priorities of God from His Word. We grow closer to God through His Word. And we also learn what God prohibits from His Word. The beginning place to really seek the will of God is through the Word of God. Does your heart reflect the Psalmist's heart, "I delight to do your will, O my God"?

Day 36

Day 36 Personal Reflection

In what ways are you seeking God's Word daily? How are you delighting in doing God's will? How are you not?

Day 37

¹⁴yet you do not know what tomorrow will bring. What is your life? For you are a mist that appears for a little time and then vanishes.
James 4:14

In today's verse, James gives some motivation for seeking God's will and not our own. The first motivation is, we have no idea what may happen tomorrow ("You do not know what tomorrow will bring"). We must make plans "in pencil."

We mustn't so set our hearts on something that it becomes a potential idol. And when life takes a different turn, we lose hope. We must have a loose grip on the things of this world and hold a tight grip on the eternal things of God. As was mentioned yesterday, planning is good, just don't put all your hope into your plans.

The second motivation James gives is the reminder that our life is but "a mist that appears for a little time and then vanishes." Like steam from a cup of tea—here one minute, gone the next.

James was not a fatalist, but he

> **We must have a loose grip on the things of this world and hold a tight grip on the eternal things of God.**

was a realist. He is not saying life is pointless. He is saying we need to remember we are only here a little while, in light of eternity, and that should affect the decisions we make.

Psalm 90 is one of only two psalms that was actually written by Moses. In v. 12, he wrote, "So teach us to number our days that we may get a heart of wisdom." We are to be wise with the little time we have on earth. Let us leverage it for things that will last for eternity. Loving God and serving others has eternal value. Our decisions should be made in light of those things.

Many people's lives reflect the lines from William Ernest Henley's poem, *Invictus*: "I am the master of my fate: I am the captain of my soul."[4] Solomon tried for many years to live like that. His conclusion in Ecclesiastes 1:2? "'Meaningless! Meaningless!' says the Teacher. 'Utterly meaningless! Everything is meaningless.'" Will you let the Lord captain your soul?

Day 37

Day 37 Personal Reflection

How are you living with eternity in mind? How are you living with God as the captain of your soul?

Day 38

¹⁵Instead you ought to say, "If the Lord wills, we will live and do this or that."
James 4:15

I'm probably not the only one who has wished God would use an audible voice to tell me what He wants me to do. It takes a lot of faith to trust in an invisible God. I believe God speaks to us today, but sometimes, I wonder if we are so busy and have so many distractions, we miss hearing the "gentle whisper" of God.

If you study the Gospels, you will discover Jesus, oftentimes, went off alone to a quiet place to hear from the Father. These moments often led to a shift in the direction or focus of ministry. Take time to seek the Lord, He wants to be found. Perhaps we are too busy striving for what we want that we aren't taking the time to say, "If the Lord wills, we will . . . "

This verse gives us room for making plans and decisions. We can make plans to "do this or that." But, the key is seeking them under the authority of God's will. I believe God's will isn't some "perfect dot" that is

> *It takes a lot of faith to trust in an invisible God.*

so easy to miss. I believe God gives lots of freedom in making decisions. I don't believe it's "Door A" or "Door B." I think God may be okay with either door!

I think God is looking for a surrendered heart; that we are truly striving to do what pleases Him. We don't need to be paralyzed in making decisions, afraid we've missed His will. Of course, if it violates Scripture or God has made it abundantly clear what He wants, then that would be the exception.

If you've prayed about it, you've made sure it isn't forbidden in Scripture, and you've sought wise counsel, then go ahead and make a decision. God's Word seems to spend more time on how to make wise decisions than in seeking to try and find some mysterious hard-to-find choice God has for us. There is freedom in Christ! A surrendered heart is already in the will of God. The question is, do you have a surrendered heart?

Day 38

Day 38 Personal Reflection

Is there an area of your life that still needs to be surrendered to God? How will you hand it over to God?

Day 39

*^{16}As it is, you boast in your arrogance.
All such boasting is evil.*
James 4:16

A person who doesn't seek God's will for their life, according to James, is a boaster. The Greek word for "boast" is *kauchaomai* and can mean "loud-mouthed." The idea is of a person celebrating their own accomplishments in such a way as to be heard by others.

Notice what the person is boasting about. They are boasting in their "arrogance." In other words, they are boasting of what they are accomplishing on their own. It reminds me of a man from the Bible, Nebuchadnezzar, the king of Babylon. He was warned, in a dream, about a great humiliation he would experience because of his prideful boasting.

And, sure enough, it happened. The king was walking on the roof of his palace, and he said, "Is not this great Babylon, which I have built by my mighty power as a royal residence and for the glory of my majesty?" (Daniel 4:30). Notice the "I"

> *Self-sufficient living is arrogant because it seeks "to play God."*

Beyond Sunday

and "my"? He was the kind of guy James was talking about.

Nebuchadnezzar went mad and lived like a beast for seven years before being restored to his position. He was singing a different tune after his seven years of humiliation. At the end of Daniel 4, he said, "Now I, Nebuchadnezzar, praise and extol and honor the King of heaven, for all his works are right and his ways are just; and those who walk in pride he is able to humble" (v. 37).

King Nebuchadnezzar went from exalting self, *to exalt the Lord*. He came to realize all he had was only possible because of God. James goes so far as to call it "evil" to *not* acknowledge and seek God in the day to day of life. Self-sufficient living is arrogant because it seeks "to play God."

You know, there is a kind of boasting we are to do. Paul tells us what it is in 1 Corinthians 1:31: "Let the one who boasts, boast in the Lord." Our boast is that we are children of God. Our boast is that God will guide us as our loving Father. Let us boast only in the Lord.

Day 39

Day 39 Personal Reflection

*In what ways might you be living self-sufficiently?
How will you boast in the Lord this week?*

Day 40

*¹⁷So whoever knows the right thing to do
and fails to do it, for him it is sin.*
James 4:17

Sin is not just doing wrong, sometimes it is not choosing to do what is right. James says if you know the right thing to do but don't, it is sin. There are sins of commission and sins of omission. You may not lie (a sin of commission), but you don't share the truth when it needs to be told (a sin of omission).

Essentially, James is giving an application to this section on God's will. He's sharing how to stop playing God. Know what is "the right thing to do" and then, start doing it! For example, if there are things at work that lack integrity, even though you aren't doing them, should you do something about it anyway? Not an easy decision, but whoever said the way of Jesus is easy?

My guess is that most, if not all, who are reading this would affirm the sovereignty of God. We would acknowledge we should follow after Jesus. But here's a challenging question that I think James was getting at: In how we

> *Sin is not just doing wrong, sometimes it is not choosing to do what is right.*

plan our day-to-day lives, are we living like practical atheists? Have we been boastful or presumptuous in how we've made plans for our lives? Are there things we know God wants us to do, and we aren't doing them?

Jesus taught that desiring and doing God's will is a mark of a true follower in Mark 3:35: "For whoever does the will of God, he is my brother and sister and mother." One of the reasons the apostle Paul accomplished so much for God's kingdom was that he was completely sold out to God and His plans.

What he wrote in Galatians 2:20 reveals this sold-out heart for God. May it be the prayer of our heart: "I have been crucified with Christ. It is no longer I who live, but Christ who lives in me. And the life I now live in the flesh I live by faith in the Son of God, who loved me and gave himself for me."

Day 40

Day 40 Personal Reflection

Is there a sin of omission you are struggling with? What does it look like in your life to be "crucified with Christ?"

Materialism and Patience
James 5:1-12

¹Come now, you rich, weep and howl for the miseries that are coming upon you. ²Your riches have rotted and your garments are moth-eaten. ³Your gold and silver have corroded, and their corrosion will be evidence against you and will eat your flesh like fire. You have laid up treasure in the last days. ⁴Behold, the wages of the laborers who mowed your fields, which you kept back by fraud, are crying out against you, and the cries of the harvesters have reached the ears of the Lord of hosts. ⁵You have lived on the earth in luxury and in self-indulgence. You have fattened your hearts in a day of slaughter. 6 You have condemned and murdered the righteous person. He does not resist you. ⁷Be patient, therefore, brothers, until the coming of the Lord. See how the farmer waits for the precious fruit of the earth, being patient about it, until it receives the early and the late rains. ⁸You also, be patient. Establish your hearts, for the coming of the Lord is at hand. ⁹Do not grumble against one another, brothers, so that you may not be judged; behold, the Judge is standing at the door. ¹⁰As an example of suffering and patience, brothers, take the prophets who spoke in the name of the Lord. ¹¹Behold, we consider those blessed who remained steadfast. You have heard of the steadfastness of Job, and you have seen the purpose of the Lord, how the Lord is compassionate and merciful. ^{12}*But above all, my brothers, do not swear, either by heaven or by earth or by any other oath, but let your "yes" be yes and your "no" be no, so that you may not fall under condemnation.*

Day 41

¹Come now, you rich, weep and howl for the miseries that are coming upon you. ²Your riches have rotted and your garments are moth-eaten. ³Your gold and silver have corroded, and their corrosion will be evidence against you and will eat your flesh like fire. You have laid up treasure in the last days.
James 5:1-3

The opening verses of James 5 contain James' strongest rebuke in his letter, which is saying something because he is not afraid to give a strong exhortation. Scripture almost presents biases that God has for the poor and needy. God is not against someone being rich, but He is against money becoming an idol and it being used to take advantage of the poor.

As mentioned in the previous chapter, "Come now" is intended to be a rebuke. This rebuke is for the "rich" (v. 1a). He states they should "weep and howl" because of the "miseries that are coming upon" them (v. 1b). The misery coming isn't because they are rich, it's because they are using their riches as a weap-

> *God refuses to play second fiddle to anything or anyone.*

Beyond Sunday

on against the less fortunate.

Remember, this letter is written to believers. Apparently, some connected to the body of Christ had an improper view of money and inappropriate use of it. God refuses to play second fiddle to anything or anyone. Jesus said in Luke 16:13, "No servant can serve two masters, for either he will hate the one and love the other, or he will be devoted to the one and despise the other. You cannot serve God and money."

When one serves money, it can lead down the path of destruction. 1 Timothy 6:10 says, "For the love of money is a root of all kinds of evils. It is through this craving that some have wandered away from the faith and pierced themselves with many pangs." The pursuit of riches can lead to ruin. And that's actually what James is getting at in vs. 2-3.

He says their punishment for loving money is that their "riches have rotted" and "garments are moth-eaten," their wealth has "corroded" and will eat their "flesh like fire." A little bit of hyperbole here, but the point is, the idol of riches will only lead to disappointment and despair.

James ends v. 3 with, "You have laid up treasure in the last days." This is very similar to what his brother Jesus said in Matthew 6:19-20, "Do not lay up for yourselves treasures on earth,
where moth and rust destroy and where thieves break in and steal, but lay up for yourselves treasures in heaven, where neither moth nor rust destroys and where thieves do not break in and steal." Let us follow the words of James and Jesus. May we live for eternal riches, not earthly ones.

Day 41

Day 41 Personal Reflection

What is an area where you struggle with the love of money? How are you being a good steward of your resources? How are you laying up treasures in heaven?

Day 42

> *⁴Behold, the wages of the laborers who mowed your fields, which you kept back by fraud, are crying out against you, and the cries of the harvesters have reached the ears of the Lord of hosts. ⁵You have lived on the earth in luxury and in self-indulgence. You have fattened your hearts in a day of slaughter. ⁶You have condemned and murdered the righteous person. He does not resist you.*
> **James 5:4-6**

In vs. 1-3, James gave an admonishment for loving money. In today's verses, we see, specifically, what the wealthy were doing wrong with it. James mentions "the laborers who mowed your fields" (4a) and "the cries of the harvesters" (4d). James says that these wealthy believers were guilty of "fraud" (4b) against their employees. Their "fraud" was that they were withholding pay to the laborers, no doubt motivated by greed and a sense of entitlement. This has no place among the body of Christ. And what a somber warning at the end of v. 4. The cries of those taken advantage of "reached the ears of the Lord of hosts."

> God sees and hears all things and He pays special attention to the needy and the helpless.

Beyond Sunday

God sees and hears all things, and He pays special attention to the needy and the helpless. God does not take it lightly when believers live a luxurious and self-indulgent life (v. 5a). It goes against the call of discipleship: "If anyone would come after me, let him deny himself and take up his cross and follow me. For whoever would save his life will lose it, but whoever loses his life for my sake will find it" (Matthew 16:24-25).

We are called to *give* not to *get*. James uses curious language at the end of v. 5: "You have fattened your hearts in a day of slaughter." What does this mean? It means they have fed their idolatrous hearts by taking advantage of the weak. And these are believers who have done it. "Day of slaughter" alludes to the coming judgment of the Lord. James is warning them they are "fattening" themselves up for judgment. Not good.

James could be referring to the unbeliever here in v. 6 persecuting, to the point of death, the righteous. And the righteous "does not resist." The righteous are willing to be persecuted for the glory of God. What a contrast. The greedy do whatever it takes to add to their wealth. The righteous, willing to suffer for the cause of Christ.

Jesus said, "For what will it profit a man if he gains the whole world and forfeits his soul? Or what shall a man give in return for his soul" (Matthew 16:26)? The righteous will be rewarded on the day of judgment. The greedy will have forfeited their souls.

Day 42

Day 42 Personal Reflection

*Do you focus more on giving or getting in your life?
Is there any greed you need to confess?*

Day 43

⁷Be patient, therefore, brothers, until the coming of the Lord. See how the farmer waits for the precious fruit of the earth, being patient about it, until it receives the early and the late rains. ⁸You also, be patient. Establish your hearts, for the coming of the Lord is at hand.
James 5:7-8

James now transitions from addressing the rich to addressing the poor. From the oppressor to the oppressed. There's a saying pastors like to say: "You need to see what the 'therefore' is there for." In other words, when you see the word "therefore" in the Bible, you need to look at the previous verses. The word "therefore" connects what was previously written in v. 4-6 where James has dealt with the rich taking advantage of the poor. Now, James is giving counsel to those who have been oppressed.

His counsel? "Be patient" (v. 7). Easier said than done when you are hurting. This is why we need the Holy Spirit in our lives, to help us do hard things. Patience is a virtue. But one that doesn't always come naturally. Often-

> *The Lord will return and right all the wrongs on this side of heaven. He will settle the score for His people.*

times, we need motivation to keep on keeping on. And James gives that motivation at the end of v. 7, "the coming of the Lord."

The Lord will return and right all the wrongs on this side of heaven. He will settle the score for His people. Romans 12:19 says, "Beloved, never avenge yourselves, but leave it to the wrath of God, for it is written, 'Vengeance is mine, I will repay, says the Lord.'"

God will also reward His people for their faithful endurance. Galatians 6:9 says, "And let us not grow weary of doing good, for in due season we will reap, if we do not give up." The return of Christ is our hope. It's what we are to live for; not for the fleeting things of this world but for the eternal glories of heaven.

James compares our waiting to a farmer. He does his part in planting the seeds, but he must wait on the Lord to bring the harvest. After he plants, the early rains come (October and November). But, as it says at the end of v. 7, he must wait for the "late rains" (March and April). Only then does the farmer see "the precious fruit of the earth."

We live in the in-between, and so, James' exhortation is to "establish your hearts" (v. 8). Stay faithful, stay focused, find joy in Christ and with His people. The day is coming when all pain and suffering is gone. All there will be is perfect joy. The return of Christ "is at hand." Jesus could return any moment. Let's find ourselves ready.

Day 43

Day 43 Personal Reflection

How are you doing with patience? What would it look like to live as if Christ might return any moment?

Day 44

⁹Do not grumble against one another, brothers, so that you may not be judged; behold, the Judge is standing at the door. ¹⁰As an example of suffering and patience, brothers, take the prophets who spoke in the name of the Lord. ¹¹Behold, we consider those blessed who remained steadfast. You have heard of the steadfastness of Job, and you have seen the purpose of the Lord, how the Lord is compassionate and merciful.
James 5:9-11

We can *get ready* or we can *grumble*. In yesterday's verses, James said we need to wait patiently for the Lord's return. Today, he challenges believers not to grumble when life is hard. The motivation, according to James, is "so that you may not be judged" because "the Judge is standing at the door" (v. 9).

Heaven will be great, but we still must give an account of our life on earth. 2 Corinthians 5:10 says, "For we must all appear before the judgment seat of Christ, so that each one may receive what is due for what he has done in the body, whether

> Pain has a way of causing us to cling to God and that's a good thing.

good or evil." James says those who "grumble against" (v. 9) each other will be judged by the Savior.

James tells the believers to look to the Old Testament prophets as role models (v. 10). They spoke and lived the truths of God's Word, and yet, some of them were persecuted for it. When we are persecuted for doing right, we stand in good company. In fact, Jesus said, "Rejoice and be glad, for your reward is great in heaven, for so they persecuted the prophets who were before you" (Matthew 5:12).

In v. 11, James mentions a number of things to consider when facing persecution for the faith. Blessed are the ones who remain steadfast. God will honor those who honor Him. Looking at the story of Job, we see God has a purpose for our suffering. God blessed Job with more than he had before his suffering. He also encountered God in a fresh new way.

And the last word of encouragement is a reminder God is "compassionate and merciful." Pain has a way of causing us to cling to God and that's a good thing. In doing so, we will discover "his mercies never come to an end; they are new every morning" (Lamentations 3:22-23). Great are You God and greatly to be praised!

Day 44

Day 44 Personal Reflection

What evidence is there that you are believing God will bless you with the painful things you are experiencing? How are you experiencing the compassion and mercy of the Lord?

Day 45

¹²But above all, my brothers, do not swear, either by heaven or by earth or by any other oath, but let your "yes" be yes and your "no" be no, so that you may not fall under condemnation.
James 5:12

Swearing oaths was a big deal in Bible times. At first glance, this verse doesn't seem to fit in the context of James' writing on being patient in painful seasons. Perhaps there is a connection. Many people bargain with God when they find themselves in a perilous situation. Many a soldier has offered up "foxhole prayers."

There are a number of topics in the book of James that correlate with the Beatitudes from Matthew 5, and today's verse is one of them. Jesus said the following about oaths in vs. 34-37, "But I say to you, Do not take an oath at all, either by heaven, for it is the throne of God, or by the earth, for it is his footstool, or by Jerusalem, for it is the city of the great King. And do not take an oath by your head, for you cannot make one hair white or black. Let what you say be simply 'Yes' or 'No'; anything

> *Consistency of character pleases God and it impacts those who see it.*

more than this comes from evil."

Jesus gave examples of things people would make an oath by, but Jesus is essentially saying that your word should be enough. You shouldn't have to swear by anything. You should be known as a person who honors your words. You do what you say you will do. James goes so far as to say that there is "condemnation" for those who don't follow through on their word.

This is really an issue of integrity. Is my "yes" really a yes and my "no" really a no? Are we truth-tellers? Are we promise-keepers? Are we people that others can rely on? Somehow, these believers, the believers referenced in James' scripture, were swearing oaths in relation to their trials and persecution. While we don't know the details, we do know that making an oath isn't necessary when in a trial.

Do the right thing. Trust in God. Don't try to bargain with God. He knows your heart, and He knows your needs. Trying to manipulate God doesn't work. Be a person of integrity, even when life is hard. Consistency of character pleases God, and it impacts those who see it.

Day 45

Day 45 Personal Reflection

In what ways are you a truth-teller and promise-keeper? How are you living with integrity, even when suffering?

_____

_____

_____

_____

_____

_____

_____

_____

_____

_____

_____

_____

_____

Prayer
James 5:13-20

[13] *Is anyone among you suffering? Let him pray. Is anyone cheerful? Let him sing praise.* [14] *Is anyone among you sick? Let him call for the elders of the church, and let them pray over him, anointing him with oil in the name of the Lord.* [15] *And the prayer of faith will save the one who is sick, and the Lord will raise him up. And if he has committed sins, he will be forgiven.* [16] *Therefore, confess your sins to one another and pray for one another, that you may be healed. The prayer of a righteous person has great power as it is working.* [17] *Elijah was a man with a nature like ours, and he prayed fervently that it might not rain, and for three years and six months it did not rain on the earth.* [18] *Then he prayed again, and heaven gave rain, and the earth bore its fruit.* [19] *My brothers, if anyone among you wanders from the truth and someone brings him back,* [20] *let him know that whoever brings back a sinner from his wandering will save his soul from death and will cover a multitude of sins.*

Day 46

> ^{13}Is anyone among you suffering? Let him pray. Is anyone cheerful? Let him sing praise. ^{14}Is anyone among you sick? Let him call for the elders of the church, and let them pray over him, anointing him with oil in the name of the Lord.
> **James 5:13-14**

As James wraps up his letter, he ends it with a challenge to be men and women of prayer. In light of all he has covered in this letter, it is only fitting to end this way. We need divine help to live out all James has taught. James also deals with various aspects of prayer.

He says we pray when we're suffering, when we're happy, when we're sick. We pray privately, we pray as a church, and we pray with other people. When Jesus was asked by His disciples how to pray, He also included various aspects of prayer. Notice what they are in Matthew 6:9-13:

"Our Father in heaven, hal-

> *Prayer shouldn't just be a laborious duty we must practice because God commands it. We must see prayer as an incredible gift from God.*

lowed be your name. Your kingdom come, your will be done, on earth as it is in heaven. Give us this day our daily bread, and forgive us our debts, as we also have forgiven our debtors. And lead us not into temptation, but deliver us from evil."

We are to praise God in prayer ("hallowed be your name"). We are to pray for God's will ("Your kingdom come"). We are to pray for needs ("Give us this day our daily bread"). We are to pray for forgiveness ("forgive us our debts"). And we are to pray for protection and help for temptation ("And lead us not into temptation, but deliver us from evil").

Are our prayers marked by the Lord's prayer? Are they marked by James' teaching on prayer? Are we praying for the suffering and the sick? Do we take time to celebrate God in prayer? Are we seeking prayer from the elders in the church? When we look at Jesus' and James' teachings on prayer, we discover prayer is something that should happen throughout the day, through the ebb and flow of life.

Prayer shouldn't just be a laborious duty we must practice because God commands it. We must see prayer as an incredible gift from God. A practice that not only draws us closer to the heart of God but helps us walk through the ups and downs of life.

Day 46

Day 46 Personal Reflection

In what ways do you need to develop a more balanced prayer life? What needs to happen to develop more vibrancy in your prayer life?

Day 47

¹⁵And the prayer of faith will save the one who is sick, and the Lord will raise him up. And if he has committed sins, he will be forgiven.
James 5:15

James challenges believers to not just pray but to have "the prayer of faith." Anyone can pray. God is looking for faith-filled prayer. Jesus often taught about the part our faith plays in seeing the movement of God. It was Jesus who said, "If you have faith like a grain of mustard seed, you will say to this mountain, 'Move from here to there,' and it will move, and nothing will be impossible for you'" (Matthew 17:20-21).

We mustn't think it is the size of our faith that leads to answers. Jesus says even a mustard seed faith works. Mustard seeds are tiny. Even an itty-bitty kind of faith will do! The point is, it's not how big our faith is, it's whether or not we have faith in a big God. Big God plus small faith can accomplish great things in prayer. Are we trusting in the God we cry out to? Do we leave our time in prayer living like God is on the throne?

> *Big God plus small faith can still accomplish great things in prayer.*

In the rest of the verse, James

gives three things that happen as a result of praying by faith. First, faith-filled prayer "will save the one who is sick." Second, "the Lord will raise him up." And third, "if he has committed sins, he will be forgiven." Let's look more specifically at these three results.

The word save in Greek is *sozo*. It is used for spiritual salvation but can also be used for physical healing. The idea here is that prayer can bring restoration to the sick. James makes it clear it is the Lord that restores ("the Lord will raise him"), not the person praying. James then says the person's sins will be forgiven.

It would seem, in this specific scenario, the person is someone who got sick because of sin. God does use sickness, sometimes, as a means of correction. 1 Corinthians 11 would be an example. The point is, prayer can lead to forgiveness of sins and restoration of health if sin is the reason a person has become sick.

The main point is to understand the power of faith-filled prayer. God doesn't always bring healing (2 Corinthians 12:7-9). God sometimes has a purpose in our pain and suffering. But, when we pray God's will and believe by faith, God moves. Are you seeing mountains moved in prayer?

Day 47

Day 47 Personal Reflection

How are you praying with confidence in light of the sovereignty of God? What "mountain-moving" prayer do you need to offer up to God?

Day 48

^{16}Therefore, confess your sins to one another and pray for one another, that you may be healed. The prayer of a righteous person has great power as it is working.
James 5:16

On this side of heaven, sin is a reality we must address. None of us are immune to it. We will hurt and be hurt by sin in our lives. We are born with a sin disease. King David wrote in Psalm 51:5: "Behold, I was brought forth in iniquity, and in sin did my mother conceive me." Paul put it this way in Romans 3:23: "for all have sinned and fall short of the glory of God."

A holy and perfect God has every right to wipe us off the face of the planet because of our sins.
But, we're told in Psalms 103:13-14, "As a father shows compassion to his children, so
the Lord shows compassion to those who fear him. For he knows our frame; he remembers that we are dust."

Oh, what words of hope! God remembers we are dust, and so, the Father shows compassion to us. We do have a part to play in our battle with sin. God shows compassion and is willing to

> God remembers that we are dust, and so the Father shows compassion to us.

forgive, but our part? Confess our sins. We ultimately confess to God, but we must also confess to one another. We need to pray for each other and our battles with sin.

We also need to confess who we've sinned against. Acknowledging our sinfulness isn't easy. But it is the path to being healed, as James puts it. Is there sin in your life to confess? Is there an apology needed to someone you have sinned against?

Returning to David's prayer in Psalm 51, David sought forgiveness for His sin with Bathsheba. We see his heart's desire in v. 10, "Create in me a clean heart, O God, and renew a right spirit within me." This is the beautiful message of the gospel. Because of the Savior's sacrifice, our sins can be forgiven, and God will create a "clean heart."

James closes out the verse by reminding us it's a righteous person's prayer that is powerful and effective. We'll look more at this in the next couple of verses, but it's a great reminder God doesn't want us to stay in our sin. He forgives us with the intent of us responding to our forgiveness with a pursuit toward righteousness.

Day 48

Day 48 Personal Reflection

How does it encourage you to know God remembers that we are dust? In what ways do you need God to help create a new heart in you?

Day 49

^{17}Elijah was a man with a nature like ours, and he prayed fervently that it might not rain, and for three years and six months it did not rain on the earth. ^{18}Then he prayed again, and heaven gave rain, and the earth bore its fruit.
James 5:17-18

The Old Testament has so many incredible examples of both men and women. If you were to put together a Top Ten of Old Testament saints, Elijah would definitely be on your list. This prophet experienced the power of God in tremendous ways.

He was fed by ravens during a famine (1 Kings 17:6). He miraculously fed a widow and her son with never-ending food (1 Kings 17:15-16). He raised the widow's son from the dead (1 Kings 17:21-23). And in a showdown, or should we say beatdown, with the prophets of Baal, Elijah prayed and a sacrifice (poured with water three times) was consumed by fire from heaven.

Elijah's name means "my God is the Lord." And because God

> *If God knows every hair on our head, He certainly knows our cares and concerns. Bring them to the Father.*

Beyond Sunday

was Lord of his life, Elijah saw the power of God unlike most people ever will. James gives another example of God's power in Elijah's life. James says in v. 17 that Elijah prayed that it might not rain. And it didn't for three and a half years!

In v. 18, it says he then prayed for rain to come and sure enough it did. Elijah demonstrated the power of God in weather. James' emphasis in these verses is that the power of God was the result of a man who prayed by faith. How about us? Are we praying by faith each day? Even if we aren't seeing the results, are we still faithfully praying?

In some ways, it might be hard to relate to Elijah. This prophet experienced the power of God unlike most in human history. I've never brought someone back from the dead. I've never created food that doesn't run out. I've never had fire come down from heaven or cause rain to stop for years. I'm pretty confident in saying that none of these things have happened in your life either.

Take comfort in knowing that God cares about the little things in our lives. The things that keep us up at night. The stuff that others may not even understand. If God knows every hair on our heads, He certainly knows our cares and concerns. Bring them to the Father. Believe by faith God will answer them in His time and His way.

Day 49

Day 49 Personal Reflection

How could you pray more faithfully even when you're not seeing results? What is God prompting you to pray more consistently about?

Day 50

> ¹⁹My brothers, if anyone among you wanders from the truth and someone brings him back, ²⁰let him know that whoever brings back a sinner from his wandering will save his soul from death and will cover a multitude of sins.
> **James 5:19-20**

James closes out the letter with a word of encouragement that doesn't seem connected to the topic of prayer. But I think it is. I think he is now talking about the importance of not only reaching out to those who "wander[s] from the truth" (v. 19) but also to pray for their return.

My guess is each of us knows people we love who have either walked away from the faith or who have never embraced the gospel in the first place. James exhorts us to do everything we can to reach out to them. But also in the broader context dealing with prayer, he is saying that we fight for the faith of others on our knees! Are you a spiritual prayer warrior fighting on your knees?

> *Eternity is at stake in people's lives. If that doesn't motivate us to prayer and action, I don't know what will.*

Beyond Sunday

James says that a person who helps bring a brother or sister back to the Lord "will save his soul from death" and also that the person "will cover a multitude of sins." We are involved in life and death things as Christ-followers. Eternity is at stake in people's lives. If that doesn't motivate us to prayer and action, I don't know what will.

The reality is, there is heaven and there is hell. We are called to help people discover the joy of knowing Christ, and with that, the path that leads to a glorious eternity in heaven. Paul wrote: "Therefore, we are ambassadors for Christ, God making his appeal through us. We implore you on behalf of Christ, be reconciled to God" (2 Corinthians 5:20).

Are we living like Christ's ambassadors? Can we honestly say that helping people find Christ is the passion and pursuit of our hearts? It's Christ's passion. 2 Peter 3:9 says, "The Lord is not slow to fulfill his promise as some count slowness, but is patient toward you, not wishing that any should perish, but that all should reach repentance."

Each of us has been forgiven of "a multitude of sins" (v. 20), and that should motivate us to help others discover that they can be too.

I hope this study has challenged you in your faith. I hope it has spurred you on to a greater passion for Christ and His Word. Like James, may we live fully and completely for our Savior. For His glory, Amen!

Day 50

Day 50 Personal Reflection

What would it look like to live fully as Christ's ambassador? Who is someone who has wandered from the faith for whom you can pray?

Notes

1. Sinatra, Frank. "Love and Marriage." Apple Music. Sony Music Entertainment, 1965. Accessed 25 November 2023. https://music.apple.com/us/song/love-and-marriage/1443167023.

2. Frost, Robert. "The Road Not Taken." Poetry Foundation, 2023, https://www.poetryfoundation.org/poems/44272/the-road-not-taken. Accessed 24 November 2023.

3. Lewis, C.S. Mere Christianity. San Francisco, Harper, 2001.

4. Henley, William Ernest. "Invictus." Poetry Foundation, 2023, https://www.poetryfoundation.org/poems/51642/invictus.

Tony Tice

Tony is husband to his beautiful bride Becky, dad to six incredible kids, and a grandpa. Tony has served as a pastor for over three decades, ministering in churches of all sizes. He presently serves as the lead pastor of a new church in northern Indiana, Church on the Rock. Tony has traveled around the world teaching God's Word. He has published numerous books, Bible studies, and devotionals. Tony's mission is to help people fall in love with the Word of God so that they will fall more in love with the God of the Word.